The Execution Culture

The Execution Culture

RESULTS HAPPEN WHERE CULTURE AND EXECUTION MEET

Chris Elias and Mark Freier

Clovercroft Publishing

The Execution Culture

©2019 by Chris Elias and Mark Freier

Published by Clovercroft Publishing, Franklin, Tennessee

Edited by OnFire Books

Copy Edit by David Brown

Cover Design by Nelly Sanchez

Interior Design by Suzanne Lawing

Printed in the United States of America

978-1-948484-98-5

Contents

Introduction

What's most important to you—culture or results?

Leaders debate this topic every decade or so. Given the recent amount of print on culture, culture seems to be the hot topic in organizations. Therefore, culture becomes a key focus for achieving results in understanding core values and implementing them throughout the entire company. Culture is important, for sure. But, we've seen companies with phenomenal cultures go out of business—because they didn't generate results.

For the past decade, we've worked with corporations across the globe to help them focus on one thing—leadership transformation through execution. After years of working with a variety of leaders, we decided to write this book to communicate what we've learned.

Any successful plan is 5 percent ideas and 95 percent execution. When you truly think about that, you can see the importance that execution plays

> Any successful plan is 5 percent ideas and 95 percent execution.

in the role of success inside any organization, no matter the industry. Unfortunately, the ability to execute is what holds most companies back from achieving their goals. Why do some companies struggle in this area? We've arrived at a simple answer: Lack of clarity. Sometimes, these companies simply haven't had the right people advising them on the steps they need to take in order to achieve their missions. Without clarity, there can be no common mission that drives results.

Getting organizations focused on execution and generating results is the differentiator. One of the tools we use is our Results Optimizer™, which combines a fully realized plan with a complete, company-wide leadership transformation in order to overcome obstacles that stand in the way of results.

In order to create a clear plan for how to move the company forward through our unique process, it is vital for leadership to recognize and address the true "elephants in the room," the issues that are present, but which no one has noticed or everyone is afraid to admit. In our initial meeting with an organization, the Nexecute® team holds what's called The Elephant Conversation™, an exploratory dialogue between our team and the organization's top leadership designed to dig into the problems or issues that stand in the way of success.

With initial clarity established, we then help them define and clearly articulate their core values. Often, organizations either have not focused on core values or have not communicated them effectively. Working together to define those core values gives companies the tools they need to both embrace and more effectively communicate those values.

Once there is a firm foundation of core values, leaders

must commit to building a culture for their company based on four essential pillars:

- Trust

- Accountability

- Engagement

- Results

Understand that this list of essential pillars is not multiple choice. You cannot choose one, two, or even three of these and expect to create a thriving, healthy culture. If your business has a high level of employee engagement and trust, yet does not deliver results, it will not grow. If your business is delivering results, but lacks trust among team members, it will not be able to sustain success. You must invest the necessary time and effort into ensuring that all four pillars are present. Do so, and your business will not only succeed—it will be exceptional.

Too often, we see organizations fail or stagnate because a leader isn't willing to invest in their culture, which translates into a lack of investing in the outcome. The sad truth is that some leaders don't consider culture as a factor in their success. Others just allow the culture to form accidentally, putting no real effort into either defining or driving the culture they want. Others may focus too much on culture and not enough on execution. At times, it can be difficult for a leader to see the forest for the trees. This is why we are here to help navigate organizational transformation.

Execution is simple to define. It is doing what needs to be done in order to achieve success. Execution functions on the basis of a plan, which is clearly defined according to the desired results. Culture, on the other hand, can feel more difficult to define and, therefore, may seem much more uncertain.

Since culture is so crucial to the success of a business, let's define what it is. Culture is an organization's values, personality, and environment. It is an accumulation of beliefs and behaviors that define and drive how people will interact within the organization. A healthy culture has a clear purpose and creates engagement. A truly distinctive culture will cause an organization to stand out in its industry. This type of culture arises within organizations and companies that have relentlessly pursued their established visions. Of course, while companies may strive to set themselves apart and create a unique culture, most do not. In order for a company to effectively create the culture required for success, there are some common elements that must be in place first.

> A truly distinctive culture will cause an organization to stand out in its industry.

Culture is the backbone of an organization. And what happens when the back breaks? You become paralyzed. You can't walk, run, or climb to the top. Once you have identified that something is broken, your first inclination may be to look at the inefficiencies, errors, or underperforming individuals on your team. However, your first move should be a re-evaluation of the core values of the culture, followed by an examination of the essential pillars. Are all four pillars in place? If not, which pillar is suffering and what actions must you take in order to restore its strength?

Was your company launched with established core values?

If it was, have you remained relentlessly dedicated to enforcing consistent alignment to those values? Or have you strayed from them, allowing them to become slogans or words on a wall somewhere? If someone asked you what your core values are, could you answer them clearly? If you've never been asked these questions before, chances are you'll need time to think about your answer.

The next question to ask is this: If you do have core values, are they the right ones? Whether you recognize it or not, core values are the genesis of everything you do. They're the reason you work hard, believe what you believe, and continue to chase your dreams. For most people, a core value is an etched-in-stone belief that drives the majority of their decisions, yet very few take the time to actually pause, define their core values, and put them in writing. This is an important step for you as a leader because it will help you understand where you're going, and how to get there. Being conscious of your core values will enable you to identify what is working, and what is not. Only then will you be empowered to make the right decisions and changes.

Identifying your specific set of core values is as important as anything you'll do as a leader. It's a jumping-off point, a foundation building exercise, and an opportunity to drill down and determine whether you're walking the talk or just talking. Often, a leader isn't interested in doing this until there has been a personal crisis and the pain from that crisis inspires them to reflect and recalibrate. Alternatively, if you choose to be proactive and identify your core values now, you will minimize the number of painful situations you will encounter.

For an organization, core values drive the mission and

unity of the team toward a common goal. The core values determine the strength and even the health of the culture, and when they're not properly defined, neither is the culture. Core values are important when building trust inside an organization. This is because the success of any relationship is directly related to the alignment of the core values of the people in the relationship. This is true among leadership teams and between peers at all levels. Differing personalities with similar core values will have a high rate of success in all relationships, both professional and personal. Conversely, similar personalities with very different core values have a high likelihood of failure.

The link between the health of an organization and the way it communicates and implements its core values is undeniable. If you want to have trusting relationships that are highly successful within an organization—a necessary component of a healthy culture—the alignment of core values is essential.

As transformation experts inside companies, the Nexecute® team is sometimes called in to help manage internal conflict within departments and teams. We've learned that when such conflicts occur, it's important to assess the perception of the culture, gain as much information as possible, and get everyone on the same page regarding organizational values. It's not uncommon to see employees who have absolutely no idea what an organization stands for, and in those cases, getting back to basics is key.

Often, this must begin with the leadership team. We help them redefine the cultural language and messages linked to core values with these questions: Who are we? What do we believe? How can we communicate to our employees that we truly care?

Every organization is filled with several different personality types and every person has their own life, dreams, personality, and internal motivators. Most people spend the majority of their time at work and desire it to be rewarding. Without clear buy-in and alignment to the company values, people will become disengaged. When they become disengaged, it's not long before they become dissatisfied and begin to question their role.

This is an incredibly dangerous state for a company. Studies have shown that disengaged or apathetic employees are not as productive as are engaged employees and can become a high flight risk, driving increased turnover. Of course, a high turnover rate will impede the organization's ability to execute plans and achieve results due to inconsistency of work, training costs, and the high long-term costs of bringing in new employees. The worst part is that this turnover will often occur among "A" players, while the "C" players stay. This costs the company even more, due to average or poor performance and the continued propagation of an accidental culture.

We wrote this book because we have a passion for helping others. Both of us have sat in the CEO chair, and have taken on the difficult challenges of creating an organization and managing the people within it. We've faced the challenges that every CEO must face—and we overcame them. We've also made our fair share of mistakes. Helping others succeed is not only critical in our daily work as organizational consultants; it's also one of our authentic core values.

There is no doubt that it is lonely at the top, and the higher you are in the leadership hierarchy, the harder it can be to find a confidant with whom to discuss the challenges you're facing. We know that leaders crave honesty and it's this authentic evaluation that allows us to guide organizations and leaders to success.

We think it's important to note that we don't identify with many of the consultants out there who haven't walked the talk of building or running a business, yet want to tell you what to do. How many times have you had a consultant sitting across from you, telling you what you need to do, and realized you weren't paying full attention? There may have been thoughts going through your head such as: "What does this person really know about my business?" or "Has this consultant ever lead a company?"

A consultant may have an MBA or even, on occasion, a PhD, but what real world, tactical business building have they really done? Have they been a career consultant, simply learning a set process based on leadership theory and applying that process to each and every client? The truth is that there are a lot of consulting companies that work this way. That's what sets us apart. Our knowledge is born from real-world experience. We have led businesses and we've walked in your shoes. Whether you're an executive or the CEO of the company, you can be assured: We have been there!

Business growth is not an easy thing to achieve and it certainly does not happen overnight or by accident. Growth occurs through intentional, evolutionary, and revolutionary changes in people and processes. We empathize with leaders as they make tough decisions because we have made those decisions ourselves.

When you have finished reading this book, it is our desire

that you will walk away with more clarity and a deeper under-standing of the next steps you need to take in the process of achieving your mission. We will inspire and encourage you to identify the alignments (and misalignments) between how you behave at work and how you behave everywhere else. We will help you gain insights into how your organization functions, versus how you want it to. Everything is connected, and our role is to partner with you on this journey and to be your trusted advisors.

CHAPTER 1

"One of the biggest mistake leaders make is they try to 'boil the ocean.' We can't do everything, so we must prioritize ruthlessly and always focus on what's most important, most critical, most impactful. Some things cannot be done right now and others may never get done, but there is always time and resources for the highest priority activities."

-CHRIS HOMEWOOD, PRESIDENT

Top Ten Execution Killers

Thomas Edison once said, "Vision without execution is hallucination." Execution is key to an organization's success, and is where most companies fall down. This is typically caused by weaknesses that slip by unnoticed in the organization. We call them Execution Killers.

Here are the Top Ten Execution Killers we have discovered. Straight talk and to the point!

WEAKNESS OF CULTURE
No Defined Culture

Throughout the years, culture has been talked about on and off and at an excessive level, but it is still the root of all problems for many organizations. Some companies have a great culture as defined by the employees, but often, when asked why the culture is so great, they only talk about the "things" the company does for them. In most of these cases, culture is defined as a bunch of tactics employed to make a great workplace. The culture in these places has an ebb and flow, depending on the manager or leader in place at that moment. These "great" great cultures are often accidental.

In most workplaces, the culture is just "okay" and in some cases even "sucks."

All of this occurs because there has never been a real effort to define the desired culture, and, even if there has been some work on it, the ongoing drive to execute the culture doesn't exist, so all the work becomes false.

To begin defining the culture, an organization must answer some key questions. The first two are "who" and "why." Who should be part of our organizational life (this includes not just employees, contractors, etc., but also customers and vendors)? And, what is our deeper purpose—why do we exist?

Who is defined by the core values? Many companies have defined their core values, but have done so incorrectly. Defining the core values is more than just sitting in a room and coming up with a bunch of words that sound great. The process should be deep and thought-provoking and will take time to finalize—in some cases up to a year. They need to be alive in the organization and so important that they would never be compromised at any cost. Because they define who should be in the organization and who shouldn't, when utilized properly, alignment of individuals occurs at such a deep level that the likelihood of relationships within the organization working is very high. This also creates an alignment that starts building a specific culture that is more than just a bunch of tactics.

To further this alignment at an even deeper level, we also need to clearly define the purpose of the organization. Some feel, especially in the for-profit world, that this is just about making money. This isn't really motivating at a deep level for most people, and though they may do their jobs and make a good salary, it doesn't support a strong culture. There may be a lot of experts and expertise, but often, there is no real energy behind their work. They may often go through life unfulfilled and looking for retirement, but not accomplishing anything that would leave a real legacy. What's saddest about these types of cultures is that often the people within them don't truly realize what they are missing.

A purpose-driven company, on the other hand, has a reason for people to be doing the work. When an individual's personal purpose is aligned with the place where they work, magic happens. People have greater energy, a more positive attitude, and much more gets accomplished in a much shorter time.

Having a clearly defined culture with Core Values and Purpose, plus other individual definitions of culture, does not allow for a purposeful approach to driving the right culture.

Not Believing Culture Matters

In his book *Boundaries for Leaders: Results, Relationships, and Being Ridiculously in Charge*, Dr. Henry Cloud reflects on culture, "You get what you create and you get what you allow." Those are poignant words for any leader. No matter how you slice it, culture matters. Rather than allowing a culture to shape itself—and by the way, when it does it will be shaped by those who are negative and/or by those who choose the "path of least resistance"—it would be incumbent on leaders to shape a desired culture. That begs the questions, "What type of culture do you want? What type of culture leads to the best execution?" We believe that there are four cornerstones or

We believe that there are four cornerstones or pillars of an execution culture.

pillars of an execution culture: a) Results driven, b) Accountability, c) Trust, and d) Engagement. Each of these pillars is important to execution. Each one takes intentional effort. Ignoring any one of them stymies execution.

WEAKNESS OF LEADERSHIP

Choosing Transactional Leadership over Transformational Leadership

Transactional leadership is a style of leadership which promotes duty based on reward and punishment. It focuses only on the transaction. So, transactional leaders ask questions like: "Did you do what I told you to do? Did you give me what I paid for?" This may seem like the path to execution. It may work for the short term but it is not a sustainable approach.

Transformational leaders know that any business is a "people business" and business is executed by and through people. Therefore, authentic leadership is leading with both your head and heart. The results are that they attract people to sacrifice perceived self-interest for a genuinely appealing collective purpose. The purpose is successful execution.

Transformational leaders practice two key principles: self-awareness and self-management. They are self-aware; they have found that while it's easier (natural, human tendency) to spend time and energy working "in" the business, WHAT they do does not matter more than WHO they are. They face the reality that 90 percent of their life is below the iceberg. They are aware of the power of story: knowing their story and wanting to learn the story of other people. They are clear about their own purpose and are driven by it. They know their own personal values and do not give in to the temptation to be liked. Rather, they genuinely serve others and have a desire to connect with people. They talk about things that inspire them and find out what inspires others. They have learned the role of EGO. They see it and because they are self-aware and self-manage, they choose to transcend their EGO.

Too Much Management and Very Little to No Leadership

Suffice it to say, this is a real issue in many companies, especially for companies that are growing fast. Simply put, when companies are smaller, the owner or head of the company must manage every aspect of the business. This soon becomes problematic, though, because the success of the company is reliant on the abilities of just one person. This is when a leader must learn to delegate, or they will just stay a manager.

The major differences between leaders and managers are as follows:

Leaders	Managers
Focus on results	Focus on tasks
Not concerned with specifics	Control the actions
Pass on and hold others accountable	Truly own the accountability
Listen, guide, and conduct	Direct and tell
Focused on long-term results	Focused on short-term deliverables
Have followers	Have robots
People are motivated to achieve	People are motivated by compensation

Here's the hard part. For many, it's much easier to manage than to lead. Psychologically speaking, this is the hardest shift a person can make during their career. Becoming a leader means changing habits, trusting others, and giving up control. Furthermore, if it isn't done right, trust is further hampered and the leader is more apt to fall back to manager mode.

When leadership doesn't exist, we also frustrate our top performers, as they aren't often given true freedom to act and get their job done. Therefore, we often say that managers have a tendency to build some form of a "robot"—people who are programmed to work a certain way and can't do anything differently unless the manager changes the programming.

Please understand, there is a time and place in every organization for a management mindset, and unlike many leadership training programs, we're not promoting that management is a bad thing. Quite the contrary, management is necessary. It's just not required for every situation. The real art is to understand how much time a person should be in leadership mode versus management mode.

For some, this shift is easy. These people understand that more can be accomplished through others than just by themselves. Many others have the ability to learn the skills necessary to make the shift, but they must have something inside of them to recognize the value of being a true leader.

Beware, though, there are others who don't possess the innate ability to become a leader. These people will not be able to make the shift. If their role is one that requires leadership, they must be moved either out of that role (and to one that is a "management" role), or out of the company.

In the end, though, the real issue revolves around delegation. True leaders will develop those on their teams to move from a position of being managed to a position of being led. This, of course, requires some work. The leader must be very clear about what results will be measured and for what the person will be held accountable. They must be willing to coach and give feedback. They must be willing to let the person to make some mistakes and learn from them. They must be willing to coach and develop the person. And, most of all, they must be able to recognize when a person isn't able to grow. For those people, the leader must be willing to act.

One important note on accountability. No one can make anyone else accountable for anything. Accountability is a choice that someone makes. Managers will try to make others accountable. Typically, a "robot" will accept this out of fear—after all, it's their boss that's telling them. The truth is, though, that their results will be severely hampered. At best, there is compliance. At worst, there will be defiance. A leader, on the other hand, engages others and will step up and accept accountability, thereby motivating and engaging their team.

WEAKNESS OF HONESTY
Not Facing Reality

It is essential to face the reality of any situation. You can't execute unless you know the starting point. We once worked with a senior leadership team who consistently missed "on-time" delivery. Every person knew it. They were frustrated by it and they were very busy trying to change the circumstance; however, they didn't talk about it as a team. After weeks (months) of posturing around the truth, a simple question was asked, "When are we going to quit ignoring the elephant in the room and face it?" Initially, there was relief, but it was quickly followed by a sense of angst: if we face this reality, we are going to have to have hard conversations and the truth will be exposed.

Not Speaking the Truth

When people are unwilling to speak the truth, they cannot change the current reality. Speaking the truth sets people free. Rather than hiding behind walls and protecting themselves, they need to face being vulnerable. This is a scary word in life and in business. After all, vulnerable comes from the Latin word "to wound." If I am vulnerable, I am exposed and, therefore, open to the fact that people could know me. Then, our inner critic fills in the blank: "I don't have all the answers, I don't have what it takes, I am not equipped for this job, I don't belong on this team, etc."

A plant manager once told us he faces invulnerability on a daily basis. He lamented that people spend so much energy keeping themselves from being "found out" that it prevents them from being their most productive. In many cases, people become paralyzed. They believe they need to have all the answers and, therefore, are unwilling to risk sharing an idea, an insight, or even calling out the truth, for fear that it will expose another team member and thereby, create conflict.

Not Ruthlessly Evaluating

There is a reason Dr. W. Edwards Deming, considered by many to be the father of modern quality control, coined the phrase PDCA (Plan-Do-Check-Adjust). There is no straight path to execution. It involves dealing with change: the circumstances of life. The Plan and Do phase is the easiest to implement; however, if you don't follow that up with the Check and Adjust phase, Checking and making the needed Adjustments, you will not execute.

We sat with a team of second tier leaders in an organization who were responsible for everything from sales to production. Their monthly concern was that, as a company, they did not Check and Adjust. Rather than systematically Checking processes, they only reacted to any emergency (sales, operations, etc.), which would occur almost daily, thereby changing the priorities. These emergencies created a constant change in focus. Therefore, the organization ran consistently in "firefighting" mode, rather than in execution mode. This was demoralizing to the employees, and it also prevented them from focusing on the priorities that would drive the company to success.

WEAKNESS OF CONSISTENCY
A Lack of Discipline

Tools are easy, discipline is hard. Many entrepreneurs seem to have some level of attention-deficit disorder, whether diagnosed or with just glaring symptoms. They tend to display levels of impulsiveness, poor time management, difficulty focusing on one thing, disorganization, restlessness, hyperactivity, moodiness, etc. Some manage these characteristics well and some do not. As the organization grows, this creates confusion and blurs the focus of the team and organization. We know of teams that say, "Here he comes again. I wonder what book he has just finished reading. Don't worry, if we just wait a while, he will either forget or be onto something different."

A lack of consistency kills culture, productivity, and most of all, execution. Leaders must have discipline to drive the culture, priorities, leadership, and everything else mentioned above. They cannot get bored with something because it is working right. They must have the discipline to continue to support and grow their people. This must all be ongoing.

As a leader fully engaged with your team, you may find yourself getting many different responses to your coaching. "It seems like I just reorganized my team. Now there are other issues I need to fix. When is it going to end?" The truthful answer is that it won't. As companies grow, so will the issues they face. The top performer last year may not be this year. The top performer today may not be so when our company has grown in the future. We've heard of glass ceilings. Everyone also has a concrete ceiling—a place where they cannot grow beyond. Leaders must have the discipline to continue to grow their teams at the pace that the company is growing.

Processes that were working in the past may become obsolete. The customer base will also continue to change. A discipline of continuous improvement must be in place. Giving up isn't an option, so leaders must have the discipline to continue. Yet, discipline is lacking everywhere.

Avoiding Accountability (or making it "soft")

Every priority in the organization must have someone responsible for its execution. Otherwise, it is simply an idea.

As we sat in on one such hour-long meeting with a senior leadership team, a General Manager repeatedly said to his team, "You gotta … (followed by something to work on)." In that one hour, we counted twenty-three times where he used the phrase, "You gotta …" Not one person wrote anything down and no name was ever mentioned to be responsible. The next month, he had another list of "You gotta …" and did not follow up on the twenty-three from the previous months.

Without accountability, there is no execution. Accountability is a two-way proposition. We cannot make anyone be accountable. On one hand, it involves a willingness to be held accountable and on the other hand, the person willing to hold the person accountable. It is the leader's job to make sure the expectations are clear, offer timely feedback, and know when and how to measure success.

WEAKNESS OF COURAGE

Not Being a Courageous Leader

Audacious leaders execute. They courageously step into situations that call for their unique strengths and carry the responsibility that comes with the position. What does it look like if leaders lack courage? First, they don't make the tough decisions. They know challenging decisions need to be made and they may even understand the consequences of not making them. But they still do not. They established workarounds. They skirt the truth. They put off what they know to be the right thing. Secondly, they are unwilling to face the fact that leadership is lonely. Leaders are ultimately responsible for execution. This is a heavy load to carry. Dealing with the nuances of the business, facing the challenges of human behavior, navigating the speed of change, and more can weigh heavily on leaders. It takes levels of courage to face it head-on. Avoiding it impacts execution.

A Lack of Courage

Execution requires action. Taking action often requires courage. It's amazing how often courage doesn't really exist. Leaders talk about it. When we ask if they are willing to do what it takes, they will often show a lot of bravado, puff out their chests, and almost act indignant at the challenge but, when it comes to acting, they often fall short. We cannot tell you how many times a leader "who is willing to fire when necessary" won't.

We have seen countless situations when, for many reasons, someone—who is toxic, misaligned to core values, is emotionally immature, etc.—is kept in place. It's obvious to everyone what should happen. However, it typically takes a major negative event for the leader to act. Why does it take something this drastic for the leader to act? We find that the decision to terminate becomes an emotional one, rather than a logical one, and the driving emotion is fear. And it's debilitating. It's damaging to the leader and it's damaging to the organization.

> Execution requires action. Taking action often requires courage.

This doesn't just show itself in firing people. It can also show itself in accountability. Anyone can set the bar low. This is easy because then they don't have to hold anyone accountable for achieving results (which takes courage). This causes less conflict and life is good. On the other hand, some (acting out of pride or meanness) will set the bar really high. Thus, when the team doesn't achieve, they can blame others for the failure—also a cowardly way to approach things. True leaders will know how to set the right bar for their team—high enough to achieve great things, but not so high that failure is guaranteed. They engage their team members and everyone (including the leader) is willing to be accountable for achieving these results. Again, this requires trust in the team to allow them to work and accomplish their goals. Trust requires courage.

WEAKNESS OF TRUST
Not Focusing on Trust

While some might make the excuse that people just want to "come to work, do their job, and go home," we know from studies and our own experience that people want to work in environments where there is a connection with other people. To connect with others there needs to be some level of trust. Therefore, the leader of any team of any size needs to focus on building trust.

What is trust? When we ask this question, we often get blank stares and the sound of crickets as an answer. When someone is brave enough to try, we often hear negative examples of trust. Therefore, we have done the work to offer teams and organizations a definition of trust to learn and live by: "a decision to let go, based on a belief that the intention and the ability of another is good."

Each phrase is important. We desire to be in control. After

all, if "I am in control, then I know it will be done right or at least my way. To let go means that I give up some control. Because I can't fully know someone, or if I do, it would take a lifetime, letting go is based on a belief." It's a decision to risk being vulnerable at some level. Yet it is not a blind risk. It is based on two essential qualities: the person's intent and ability. This affords a leader the opportunity to make a choice and not be a victim. They can make a judgment call on the person's intent. Do they think it's good and aligns with the core values of the organization, or do they think and believe that the person is out only for themselves? Not only do they get to make a judgment call on their intent, they can also evaluate their ability. People prove themselves more trustworthy over time. The more a person is trustworthy, the more you can risk letting go. Trust is a gift. The more a leader trusts, the more they can let go. If two people are new to a relationship or if someone has withdrawn a lot of trust from our trust account, they will be less willing to give up control and will be more measured until a deeper level of trust is established. This may sound like it takes work. It does. And it is worth it.

A Lack of Trust

The root of all team functionality is trust. The challenge is to move the continuum from an absence of trust to an abundance of trust. Let's be clear that team trust is actually trusting *people*. There must be trust between individuals and throughout the company. If work isn't being done to support the desired culture on a continuous basis, trust won't exist throughout the company. Core values alignment is necessary, or the ability for trust to exist is severely impeded. Even though everyone wants to have this, very few are willing to do what it takes to get there.

Courage is key here. Are we willing to do what it takes? If there is a person that is toxic to the organization, are we truly willing to confront them and potentially terminate them? When this doesn't happen, trust breaks with those who expect the leader to hold others to a high standard.

How about listening? Does the leader truly listen to their people and take into account what they say? Or, are they and their words dismissed? To get to a place where people in any organization are engaged, truly listening, and taking others' thoughts into account is essential. Teams must be able to engage in conflict and debate to get to root issues.

Every leader wants their people to be fully engaged. This doesn't happen unless they feel that they can participate, contribute, and are heard. To let them do this takes courage and most of all, trust.

WEAKNESS OF EMPLOYEE RELATIONSHIPS

Not Engaging People

At first glance, engagement may seem "squishy." This couldn't be further from the truth. At its core, engagement is harnessing people holistically to express themselves and drive the overall performance of the organization. As one of our Four Pillars of Culture, it is not mutually exclusive from execution. Rather, it is an integral component toward execution. Engaged people who execute have a sense that their job matters; they are having an impact on the success in the organization, and as people, they matter.

Engaging people has many layers. It involves decisions in hiring the right people, people who are aligned to the core values. It means making sure that the right people are in the right seats on the bus, and understanding each person's unique strengths and weaknesses. It means properly training them in WHAT they bring to the organization—playing to strengths and managing weaknesses so that they can partner better with others—and WHO they are as people and what it means for the organization. It means being consistent in cascading the right messages so that priorities are on point. It also means making the tough call to be sure people's behaviors are aligned to the core values and to release people who do not align to the core values. People want to make sure that the organization does not lose sight of the vision or only be focused on chasing money. This provides some stability for them and builds a sense of hope. Finally, it means telling people the truth.

Hiring the Wrong People

Most companies have terrible hiring practices and hire the wrong way. Typically, they would build a job description with only the skills and experience necessary for the job, then begin the hiring procedure based on this. They recruit and get a bunch of resumes, select a handful, and begin interviewing. Often the complete interview process revolves around asking questions to validate their resume. In the end, they select the one that feels right to them. Hopefully, this will work.

Sometimes companies will employ some sort of assessment process to help determine fit (both cognitive and personality).

But what assessment to use is the key question. There are dozens of assessments on the market. Yet, do they really work in hiring the right employee for the job?

We find that companies are looking for the silver bullet of hiring. This may sound harsh but it's a bit like buying snake oil in the old days. They believe that using an assessment is the answer. Assuming the company is using one of the few truly validated assessments on the market, they still need to beware of what the assessment tells them. It should only be used for additional information and not be a basis of decision. Those that utilize assessments must also be aware of what type of assessment they are using.

Except for one assessment on the market, all assessments measure either the cognitive or affective portions of the mind. Cognitive assessments are fine for determining if a person has the minimum intelligence required for getting the job done, but have no real correlation or ability to measure future job success. Affective assessments—which measure emotions, personality, values, etc.—have their place. Though there are some that have been around for many years, because they measure emotional states and stability, they can be affected by many situations and may or not be accurate—they boast they are. We know of cases where people have manipulated their results to look a certain way through their answers. We also know that these can change over a lifetime—especially for individuals that don't have a strong result in a particular area.

Organizations that have evolved to the next level will employ behavioral interviewing techniques. This increases the chance for success, but not if it is only focused on skill and experience, which is, again, how most companies do it.

This type of process is severely flawed and backward. To hire properly, companies must look at core values, as well as personality and cognitive fit. And, they must be looked at in this order.

As discussed before, it starts with the job description, but it must have much more than just the skills and experience needed. At the top of every job description, there should be the company's core values. Next, any personality traits necessary to fit in the company should be listed along with specific personality traits necessary to be successful in the specific role (e.g., you don't want a highly introverted person in sales). Finally, comes the cognitive stuff. This is not just the skills and experience, though. There needs to be a clear definition of what the person will be specifically accountable for, what results are expected in the role, and how those results will be measured.

From there, the process should go like this:

1. An accurate description of the job is posted.

2. Resumes are reviewed to ensure the candidates that will be interviewed have the experience and skills to do the job.

3. Initial phone interviews are conducted to either qualify or disqualify candidates to ensure that only good candidates will go through the formal interview process.

4. Qualified candidates are identified and invited for formal interviews.

5. And now the MOST important part—Behavioral interviewing is utilized in all the interviews to clearly determine if the candidates have the core values.

6. As candidates are identified that have true alignment to the core values, personality assessments (if utilized) are used and those who qualify go through a resume qualification process to ensure they didn't lie on their resume—which, if they have the core values, shouldn't be an issue. Note: Though there will naturally be some skills validation in all the interviews, every interview must have some form of core values validation process.

7. A final interview on job offers only go out to people that have the core values and have had their skills validated.

It's important to avoid the temptation of becoming enamored with a candidate for the wrong reasons. Perhaps they are like us, or we just like them, or their resume is so strong that we want them at all costs. This happens often and these candidates get preferential treatment in the process, often leading them to being the one hired. This can be disastrous for everyone involved, including the candidate.

The only way to solve this is to have a clear process for hiring people who have a high potential for success in the organization and taking our feelings out of it. You must have someone who is a great relationship fit, personality fit, and cognitive fit for your organization.

Keeping the Wrong People

There is an old saying: "Hire slow and fire fast!" Yet companies don't seem to do either. As mentioned above, their hiring process may be flawed, and often they are in a hurry, so the wrong person is hired, but then what? It's amazing how often people are kept around for long periods of time when they have been identified as being the wrong person. This is very costly, not just financially, but from a results and emotional standpoint.

When evaluating people, multiple criteria must be utilized and the criteria must be as objective as possible. All too often, measurement criteria are subjective—not tied to real goals or metrics—and can be arbitrary. Under those circumstances, how can you really know if people are any good? This can give a manager an excuse and allow them to keep people around for the wrong reasons.

We must ensure that three essential categories of performance are continuously measured and evaluated (in this area): 1) core values/cultural fit alignment; 2) performance against specific and clear goals; and 3) future potential.

If at any point the person is deemed to not have the core values of the company, they must be moved out as soon as possible. Core values can't be fixed or trained. If they don't have them, they never will. If a person doesn't have the core values and they are in the company, there are opportunities for disruptions in many forms, ranging from poor communication to outright fights between people. Suffice it to say, if the core values aren't there, they won't play well with others.

There are other cultural fit items which must be evaluated, including emotional, behavioral, and personality traits. Though people can learn to become more emotionally healthy, which will impact their attitudes and behavior, this takes a lot of work and investment. It is often not worth it, though many managers and leaders will try to change people. Constant monitoring and evaluation is needed and if change isn't happening, the person must be moved out of the organization.

Lastly, how are they performing against their goals? Assuming the first two evaluation points are fine, if they aren't performing, they need to be put on some form of corrective action or moved to a role where they can perform.

If there are low standards, how can you know if someone is a good fit? If there are high standards and the leader doesn't act, then the company's future success is impeded. In all these scenarios, the problem is that leaders and managers hold onto the wrong people way too long and in the process either lose good people or, at a minimum, lose productivity.

WEAKNESS OF TEAMWORK

No Real Teams Exist (Only Workgroups)

As many of these execution killers begin to overlap, another to be recognized is the lack of any real teams. To understand this, we must first understand what a team is. We define a team as a group of people who come together for a long period of time to achieve a set of results. These results are ongoing and grow over time, and the team must continue to strive for growth and achievement. Though each member of the team has a certain amount of independence—each has a specific area that they are in charge of—there must also be a high amount of interdependence. Each member of a team must rely on others on the team to execute their job and help in achieving team goals, or the team fails. Teams must be led and run by a leader—again, one who functions with leadership mindset.

Contrary to a team is a workgroup. These are a group of individuals who come together for a specific task and to achieve a specific result. Once that result is achieved, the group is no longer needed, though members of the group may work together again on something else, but that would be separate from work they have done before. Each person brings a specific expertise and are very independent. There is little to no need for interdependence, and it often doesn't exist. Workgroups are run by managers who control all aspects of the work the group is doing.

In an organization, teams at various levels are necessary. The problem is that they don't truly exist where they should. It is often the case that these supposed teams are being run like workgroups. Often the person in charge acts like a manager, e.g., more focused on tasks and controlling the action than helping achieve results. Furthermore, meetings look more like report outs and there is no real interchange of information or group problem solving.

Because they are managed this way, there is little trust, engagement, and accountability. The result is that the ability to maximize potential is impeded. Lower standards are usually set so the group can feel accomplishment, as opposed to setting high standards and driving the group to work together and achieve more.

WEAKNESS OF PRODUCTIVITY
Being Busy Kills Productivity

It's repeated like a broken record: "We are just too busy!" It's followed closely with the question, "How am I supposed to get anything done?" The growth in technology and speed of information is driving us to act faster and faster. The common complaint among teammates is that people don't respond to emails fast enough. In the midst of this busyness, we are losing sight of what productivity really means.

We often ask how many items an individual has on their "to do" list. The answers we get range from thirty-five to 150 plus. Really? 150 plus? How do they get anything done? Productivity is about understanding what's most important at any time. It's about efficiency. If a person is choosing busy over being productive, the default actions when looking at the to-do list are either based on what's easiest or the most burning or painful issue of the moment. Neither activity is very productive.

We learn from watching and listening. Learning about the difference between productivity and busyness came in the form of a basketball player who played basketball at UCLA under legendary coach John Wooden. One day before practice, as Wooden was checking in on the players, that particular player was lamenting about how busy he was. Wooden let him share for a minute or so and then interrupted him with the question, "It really doesn't matter how busy you are. Were you productive?" There is more than a nuance difference between the two.

For a person to be productive, you first need to understand the priorities. Once you know what is important, you schedule around the priorities and work on them, thus ensuring good, productive forward progress. Unfortunately, it's not just that simple. If the priority is always the biggest pain point or issue that has just cropped up, then we aren't doing a good job of identifying priorities soon enough.

This is the way we teach it: when looking at your day, week, month, quarter, year, or life, ask this question: "If I could only do one to three things today (or this week, month, quarter, etc.), what would take me further than anything else toward

> "It really doesn't matter how busy you are. Were you productive?"

reaching my goal?" If leaders could build habits around this type of thinking, then the forward motion of their work in the organization would improve greatly; therefore, they would be executing.

So, the next question arises: what is a real priority? It's no surprise that under different situations, different types of priorities might be chosen. In some situations, leaders may identify the wrong priorities, thus having a negative long-term effect on their company.

Two examples of this exist in companies that are being packaged for a sale and companies that are in a turnaround. For companies that are in a turnaround, daily stresses drive decision making on priorities. These companies live day-to-day, hoping to get out of their mess. Though these companies shouldn't be considering ten- to twenty-year goals, they should be looking at both ninety-day and twelve-month goal setting. These goals should ensure they are moving through the turnaround in a productive manner. If they are only focused on daily goals and living to tomorrow, that's all they will get. A bankruptcy is on the horizon for them. A true turnaround for them will not only include some longer-term vision and goal setting, but also the courage to make the right decisions about people.

It's also amazing to us how many companies, when the decision is made to sell, will start making decisions for the wrong reasons. The inexperienced leader will make the ultimate priority the amount of money they will make on the sale. They will look at profits, EBITs, and other financial indicators, but they don't truly understand the concept of "the multiple." This is about how many times the profit or EBIT a purchaser is willing to pay. Most sellers also make the mistake of believing that a sale will occur faster than it really will.

As they make profits their priority, they start making short-term decisions to try to drive that number. These decisions can include cutting training, marketing, and other costs that are essential to long-term success, even though they might not be needed in the immediate short term. Savvy buyers will recognize this. They will understand that these are costs that will be added back in later and when an offer is made, this will be usually seen in the multiple being offered—say as low as 1x to 1.5x profits, as opposed to something much higher. Also, if a sale takes longer than anticipated, the profits will be negatively affected because of the lack of the things that were cut that were part of the success in the first place. The result: lower profits + lower multiple = very low sale price.

When selling a company, the leadership of the company must continue to operate the company like they will have it for an additional twenty years. This forces them to stay engaged and continue to grow the company. This will prove that there is a real value for a buyer and will show in the multiple. Companies we have worked with have seen multiples of 8x or greater by being great.

One company we worked with decided they wanted to

tell a story of continued growth. Though the owners had an exit plan two years out, they focused on continuing to do the things that worked for them in the past. They kept growing their people, they reinforced their culture, and they continued to drive to a long-term goal which was set for ten years in the future. Over the next couple of years, they were able to improve their EBIT from 9 percent to 28 percent. This allowed for an even bigger win for them. Not only could they get a bigger multiple, the number being multiplied was even greater, having a huge positive effect on their company's value.

On the other hand, we were privy to an organization which decided to focus on the "sale" and not focus on building and maintaining a culture of execution. The conversations at every level were about how every decision and every process would impact the sale of the company. Profits became the driving motivator. People and programs were cut, as well as budgets across the board, all with the intent of making the bottom line look better. Not only is this exhausting, it is demotivating. Quarterly priorities were slowly ignored and eventually abandoned. Leadership mindsets, again at every level of the organization, were exchanged for manager mindsets—leading to micromanaging conversations with clients, purchasing, etc. Accountabilities around core values stopped. Trust eroded at rapid rates. We would hear from midlevel managers, "Doesn't corporate realize what they are doing to the long-term growth? They are driving good people away!" Now, here's the real problem. A potential buyer didn't materialize as fast as the organization thought it would. The cuts they made, while having a short-term impact on profits, started to impact their ability to sell. By the time that some buyers started coming to the table, the organization had a reduction of over 20 percent in sales, as well as a negative impact on their EBIT. This gave the impression to buyers that the management of the company didn't know how to run a company, which changed the complexion of the offers. When offers did come in, they were much lower than expected or desired.

Lastly, let's talk about data. Every company we come across looks to employee data. But are they looking at the right data and are they making data-based versus gut-based decisions? We have seen too many companies looking at the wrong data. In some cases, they don't have enough data and in others they overdo it, generating so much data that it becomes impossible to know what's relevant. How can you determine your priorities and what would be most productive without good data? Organizations must look beyond the standards and determine what data will drive the best decision-making. They then need to get this data on a highly visible and visual dashboard and this dashboard should be utilized daily to drive tactics and strategies to move the organizations forward.

WEAKNESS OF RESULTS
Not Acting Like Results Matter

That may sound harsh, but let's face it. Words are cheap. Leaders can say they believe in results, but actions will reveal the true belief. If leaders truly believe that results matter, they will make sure that every action is geared to getting results. They will be very clear about the top priorities and assure that every department and team drives their actions to accomplishing these priorities. They will implement a system of regular disciplines—Meeting Rhythms—to ensure that the right data is being recorded. In this way, right actions are celebrated and the obstacles are being addressed and corrected in fashion. Leaders know that the "little things" matter. Consistently missing on the "little things" will lead to an accumulative larger issue. By making sure that the culture is results driven, it also sends the clear message that being productive is more important than being busy and that being productive means focusing the right energy on the right actions that will yield the right results.

Broken Processes or
No Processes That Drive Results

It's been said, "I'd rather be lucky than good." Any leader (or manager for that matter) who says that is short-sighted and narrow-minded. Processes are essential to identify where issues are and to replicate successes. This takes work and will force some into making decisions. It will also feel like taking away the freedom from some.

For companies to execute at the highest levels, the guesswork has to be removed. Guesswork is fine as part of the visioning process but is too ambiguous when it comes to getting things done. So, a process needs to be in place for everything. The truth is that often many processes exist, but they may have never been formalized. Furthermore, not enough people understand them, so it becomes difficult to improve.

Great companies don't only identify processes, but understand process flow, critical points, and handoffs, so that when something doesn't work right, they can isolate the issue and fix it. The best processes are the ones that have been modified and adjusted enough times that they work close to flawlessly. They become a habit for the people executing the process, which, in turn, ensures maximization of results.

CHAPTER 2

"Companies must be both strong and smart. Every business needs strategy and a culture that drives execution. The strategy is the easy part. A culture of execution retuires intense focus and discipline."

- PATRICK DAVIDSON, VICE PRESIDENT

The Importance of Culture Plus Execution to Drive Results

Have you ever observed an organization that didn't seem aligned in its culture? *It is not enough to have a great culture alone.* As we've said before, a great culture and excellent execution must coexist. You can't have one and not the other and get positive results. You might get results, but not the ones you want. *Culture is an important factor in driving execution.*

How do you define this core culture?

CLARITY

Organizations need clarity in their culture and processes. This first step brings a high level of clarity that gets everyone on the same page. It's the starting point for success. Without clarity, there can be no progress. But how do you achieve clarity when there are so many initiatives, processes, teams, and leaders? It's not uncommon to have a lack of clarity on cultural messaging and vision, due to a lack of continuous and positive reinforcement and communication about the culture, vision of the company, and the overall goals.

Clarity impacts culture and execution.

It is up to the leader to establish the vision and create clarity within the organization. When a leader establishes clarity, it becomes easier for everyone to make decisions from the core goal of the organization. Ford Motor Company CEO Mark Fields established the company's goal of moving into technology to keep up with competition. Ford posted revenues in excess of $149 billion in 2016 and is a leading force on the Fortune 500 list. They had been in talks with companies like Google and Uber, but decided not to partner with either, as Mark Fields said that company culture was a big driver.

How can an organization keep up with changing technology and competition?

> The key to disarming these land mines is to uncover any cultural blind spots or misconceptions and get everyone aligned toward a desired company culture and vision.

At times, leaders are aware of problems or challenges that exist in the marketplace, yet they are unaware of the issues and land mines that exist beneath the surface. The key to disarming these land mines is to uncover any cultural blindspots or misconceptions and get everyone aligned toward a desired company culture and vision. Once everyone is aligned, a stronger culture will support a more cohesive mission and teams that execute and drive consistent results.

Every organization is made up of a diverse array of people with separate lives, dreams, personalities, and values. They invest a lot of their time at work and want that time to be rewarding. Without clear buy-in and alignment to the company's culture, people will become disengaged and see their work as "just a job." When this occurs, they are bound to be dissatisfied and won't connect well with their coworkers. When disengagement seeps into a culture, it can spread resentment, apathy, and anger, leading to disastrous results.

Take the following as an example. One of our clients became the new general manager of a $12 million manufacturing company. The sales were dismal, the on-time delivery was less than 40 percent, and the employees at every level were defensive and fearful. They were "led"—we use that term loosely—by a command-and-control leader. The senior leaders didn't trust each other and it leaked throughout the plant. It was a spiral of negativity. The results of the employee survey were horrendous.

For the first forty-five days, the new GM watched and listened. He didn't make a single change. On day forty-six, he gathered the senior leaders and pointed to the core values on the wall of the conference room. They had never been referred to in the past. Safe to say, not one leader knew what they meant and how to lead with them. The GM made a simple statement, "From this moment, the purpose of the organization will be the centerpiece and the core values the guiding principles by which we make every decision. And, I mean every decision."

Like most long-term employees, the senior leaders thought he was "blowing smoke" and this "flavor of the day" would pass. It didn't. Why? Because the leader was relentless in his commitment to the core values and consistently communicating them at every meeting, every one-to-one, and every town hall. He ruthlessly held leaders accountable to them. Behaviors were established around the core values and behavioral interview questions became part of the hiring process. Within a few months, leaders and long-term employees were removed who did not align to the core values. Word got out that the GM was serious. You see, the GM committed to following a business strategy based on the right priorities, following the right plan, while building the right environment and hiring and promoting the right people. By the way, in his words, "After fifty years in business, we have grown 150 percent in three years (as an organization that has been in business more than fifty years, that is unheard of), and have done so while growing more aligned, and producing more raving fans as customers."

One of the challenges to a healthy culture is consistency and communication.

Each of those personality types in your organization or any company receives communication differently and has differing belief systems and values. How do you reach each of them with the same consistent message to bring all of the individuals together and laser-focused on the same culture and the same mission?

Culture is an organization's values, personality, and environment. It is an accumulation of beliefs and behaviors which define and drive how people will interact within the organization. When right, it has a clear purpose and creates engagement.

So, how is it established? With clarity and intent.

But of course, as any seasoned leader knows, it's not quite

as simple as that. It truly starts with defining the desired culture, then being purposeful and relentless in doing everything necessary to drive the essential pieces that support the desired culture and eliminating those that work against it. Though many companies strive to have a unique culture, there are some common elements that must be in place first.

Like creating a building, you must first have a solid foundation. This doesn't happen overnight. Next, you set your pillars on the foundation, which supports everything else. From there, you can make your building look and function any way you like. Culture impacts and drives execution. In our roles as CEOs and consultants, we've helped communicate culture to the leaders inside organizations, and it all comes down to the process below:

Foundation → Pillars → Unique (Desired) Company Traits → Culture

To fully understand this flow, let's start at the beginning and clarify what makes up the Foundation and Pillars of Culture. We have to first understand what determines an organization's cornerstone and define the pillars of an organization.

The formula is: Foundation + Pillars = Culture.

THE FOUNDATION

The first ingredient is the Foundation of culture, or if you like to conceptualize in terms of shapes, the base of your organization's pyramid is the organization's core ideology. This is a combination of its core values and purpose. The leaders in any organization should be able to answer the questions "who?" and "why?"

If everyone within the organization held the same values and truly bought into the organization's purpose, their ability to work together would be maximized, allowing them to strive toward the same goals and hold each other accountable to the same standards.

Without a core ideology, it becomes much more difficult for relationships to succeed. When that occurs, the daily and consistent focus on what's important gets blurry and individuals can become task-oriented managers, or "all about themselves."

When you begin working with a client, they will always assure you they have clearly stated their core values to the company. One such client even explained they had weekly huddles where the values were talked about and people aligned with them. They were printed in a binder in the lobby. For context, this is a great organization with great people at every level. The owners are passionate and empowering servant leaders. At our first meeting, the senior leadership team had us almost convinced that we didn't need to address their core values. But something didn't seem right.

We believe that an organization should never have more than three to five core values and they had ten. Too many core values creates a lack of clarity and it also creates a problem with knowing your team truly knows and embraces these values. We asked the senior leaders to do an exercise. Let's test their knowledge of what they were very certain were understood values. We asked them to write out all ten core values. After five minutes, you could tell they were not going to manage all ten. "What are all ten of the core values?" Not one of them had ten. Most had five or less. Not even the owners could list all ten.

Why? Not because the ten weren't good principles. Ten is too many. And the ten were not core values. We then embarked on a six-month process to identify, test, and artic-ulate five core values. Today every leader knows what each value means and the specific behaviors around which they, as leaders, will hire, promote, encourage, hold accountable, and if need be fire their people. The new core values made sense for the organization and more importantly, every employee applauds them because they provided boundaries for the organization. The senior leaders now say, "These values are US! This is WHO we are!"

We once started working with a leadership team in a large manufacturing plant of a Tier 1 supplier for automotives. They were a competitive bunch, in part because the GM loved competition and, therefore, assembled high-performing, competitive individuals to be leaders. His struggle was that they weren't acting like a team. On one level, they were mak-ing the numbers. At another level, they operated in silos. After a few months, we asked them about their core values. They looked quizzically and said that they honestly never thought about them, or for that matter, knew them. A couple of them referred to the poster on the wall with the purpose and core values and another said, "I don't even know what they mean."

At that point, the new HR manager said, "I have a PPT slide deck with the core values listed, explained, and even behaviors that are expected around each core value." No one in the room knew what she was talking about except the GM. You see, "corporate" spent a lot of money identifying and clarifying the core values. There are only five and they are excellent. Yet, "corporate" did not communicate them well or reinforce them to the leaders nor the hourly employees. Hundreds of people came to work every day to complete a job. They weren't given boundaries around which to perform, attitudes around which to align, or an environment in which they could contribute in a meaningful way. They missed the core values. The plant made money. Numbers were met. Yet, the very foundation of the organization, the core values, remained in a poster on the wall or a PPT slide instead of in the heads and hearts of the employees. To change that, we had to start with the leaders.

They may develop tunnel vision in pursuit of their own biased and personal core values, counter to the agenda of the team's at large, or even become focused on burning others' platforms, as opposed to the collective success of the organization.

A few years ago, we had a situation where we were asked to come in and coach a member of an executive team who wasn't getting along with anyone else. The situation had degraded to the point where he was losing members of his group at an alarming rate and no one else on the executive team wanted to deal with him. He was hired for his expertise, not his fit to the organization. As a matter of fact, the CEO didn't want to hire him, but he had a big technical issue and his board made him hire the candidate with the most credentials. The company then had to spend a considerable amount of money buying him out of his contract and relocating him. They also had to pay a signing bonus (this should have been a big red flag). Within six months, he had lost half of his team and more were threatening to leave. We began the coaching process and it was obvious in the first session that he didn't have any of the company's core values and wasn't willing to work with others. He couldn't care less if his relationships with others was toxic and didn't realize the impediment this was causing to his success. From his point of view, everyone else was wrong. The CEO had no choice but to fire him, which was costly, as they had to buy him out of the contract they gave him and relocate him back to his home city. All because they hired for skills versus core values fit. It's relatively easy to find people with skills, but cultural fit is hard. We should look at that first and then qualify the skills.

We had another client situation where there was an executive that seemed to be a great fit. He appeared to have a lot of positive energy, but one day, during a good news check-in at the beginning of a meeting, we noticed that nobody was paying attention to his good news. This was a big red flag that the other team members didn't care and potentially didn't trust him. Upon further investigation, we discovered that he was perceived as a bully. The culture of this company was very calm and a very gregarious person was not a good fit to the values or culture. Mind you, we don't judge whether someone is a good or bad person based on their values and behaviors, but instead consider whether they are a good or bad fit for the company. In a follow-up conversation, the CEO and he decided that he would be better off somewhere else. We coached him on how to find a core values fit for himself when looking to join an organization and he found one that was a good fit. He is happier and more successful being in a place where he is a good fit.

When the core values aren't in place or enforced, relationships sour and often, fail. Worse yet, the good people—the right people—eventually leave and the culture becomes more toxic. Team alignment is a critical aspect to success and execution. Think of establishing the core values and purpose of your organization as the basis of alignment for the entire organization. This includes the leadership, management, and team members alike.

The second ingredient is those four pillars of any organization.

THE FOUR PILLARS

Results – Without results, where would we be? As much as we might want to focus on everyone's happiness, we're still in a business and we need results to help keep us afloat. While results are nonnegotiable, how we achieve them is up for debate.

Accountability – An organization cannot function if team members are constantly pointing fingers and arguing over whose job is what. Accountability means taking ownership and taking pride in the success of your organization, projects, or processes.

Engagement – Team members not engaged in an organization's purpose and goals might as well be an empty desk chair. They may be doing their job but are they invested in the overall success of their role? What about the growth, security, and results of the entire organization?

Trust – Most leaders know that trust needs to be a pillar. However, trust doesn't just happen. Trust must be intention-

> Team members not engaged in an organization's purpose and goals might as well be an empty desk chair.

ally developed. It starts with having a clear definition and understanding of trust. It is nurtured through individual vulnerability and honest, often hard, conversations. It is a decision to make and a skill that is developed.

Once you have the foundation and these four pillars defined, you can identify other unique aspects of culture for your company and start developing strategies to drive your culture.

CHAPTER 3

"Core Values are paramount to the foundation of a strong, great organization. We have learned to not only hire for Core Values, but also evaluate staff for Core Values and sometimes terminate for Core Values. If organizations don't operate through the lens of Core Values, they're on a slippery slope to, at best, be dysfunctional and ultimately collapse."

-DEBORA MATTHEWS, PRESIDENT AND CEO

Core Values and How They Impact an Organization

What should the basis of an organization be? An organization's core ideology is the basis of its culture. We must never forget that a strong foundation is a necessary building block for all structures. A weak foundation will crumble, causing everything that's built upon it to crumble along with it. Built on the foundation are the four pillars of a culture. We call them pillars because without these four supports, the structure of the organization could crumble. Every organization must have these. Once this is defined for an organization, the other elements of culture are built upon them.

Core values define who should be in the company and who shouldn't. It is the people in the company that define the culture. If their core values align with the company, that is when we have a really nice culture. When we don't create core values that we are willing to hire and fire by, then we create an accidental culture that we may not want. The more alignment we have at a core value level, the more accurate our culture will be and the more directed our work.

Every organization has the same core challenges. When we implement programs to overcome people challenges or issues with systems or processes or culture, we focus on the foundation first. The foundation of the company plus the pillars and core values equals the culture that company demonstrates.

THE INITIAL SET OF CORE VALUES

When an organization is founded by one person, or a partnership, or even a small group of people, it adopts the core values that one person holds or that this close group of people share. This process is only natural. This is why separation can also occur between internal organizational departments that have two very different leaders with different values. Ultimately an organization should hire and promote people that are aligned with their core values.

While we could cite many examples of organizations who know their core values and hire and promote people who are aligned with their core values, let's take a high-level look at Chick-fil-A. Regardless of how you feel about their overall purpose, they set the standard of how to live out their core values. It is no accident that lines are extraordinarily long at every Chick-fil-A around the country at meal time. It is not an accident that you are greeted at the drive-through or in the store with a pleasant greeting and an introduction of the name of the person taking your order. It is no accident that most of the time the entire experience is a pleasant one for the customer. Why? Their first core value is Customer First. Truett

Cathy, Chick-fil-A founder, said it years ago, "We can change lives by the way we treat people."

How does that happen? By focusing on every core value: Personal Excellence, Continuous Improvement, and Working Together. In most cases, at least three people are talking or relating to you in your customer experience. Employees are trained and held accountable to the Core Four of Relational Leadership: 1) make eye contact, 2) smile, 3) speak enthusiastically, and 4) stay connected. (Please know that we are getting no endorsement money from Chick-fil-A and in the future will continue to wait in line like the rest of you.) What we want to highlight for you is the intentionality of having clear core values and the process to embed them into your organization.

Parenthetically, at other businesses when you experience poor customer service, no eye contact, no smiles, or people not taking pride in themselves, it is no accident. That behavior is allowed! The fault lies squarely with the senior leaders who let it happen. You may give them return business, but it's only because they have a corner on that particular market.

Similarly a charge nurse once shared her dilemma with us. She tried to function as a leader and knew all three shifts were struggling because of a bad culture in her department. Nurses were on their cell phones, not completing tasks, and had poor attitudes. She saw herself as a leader and wanted to change the culture, and nothing she tried seemed to make a difference. At a meeting with the other charge nurses and the nurse manager, she brought up the challenge and the idea of "write-ups" was suggested as an option. The nurse manager then asked the other charge nurses if they were willing to hold their people accountable and start writing them up. They responded with,

"No!" That meant nothing changed. The culture remains the same. In fact, it becomes even more toxic over time. The rest of the fallout will be that patient care will suffer and the "A" players will eventually leave.

It didn't start that way. When people start businesses from the ground up, they are pouring their heart and soul—blood, sweat, and tears—into their work. Every piece of what's important to them, what drives them, and what they value is instilled in their new organization. Why shouldn't their work reflect what's important to them? Identifying these values and traits have been built into the very foundation of the organization. This can be a challenge to maintain as an organization grows.

What starts to happen as the organization begins to grow rapidly and that cornerstone needs to be built upon?

CORE VALUES

Core values are important when building trust in an organization. We believe the success of any relationship is directly related to the core values of the people in the relationship. Differing personalities with similar core values will have a high rate of success. Similar personalities with different core values at their roots have a very high likelihood of failure. If you want to have relationships that are highly successful within an organization, which is the foundation of having a culture of trust, the alignment of core values becomes essential. The way to do it is to identify company core values through a discovery process, and hire and fire people based on those core values. This foundation can extend to good clients and bad clients based on the alignment of values between people.

Core values can be similar in different companies, but the combination of core values creates uniqueness for your company. Parenthetically, we actually practice what we preach. Before we became partners, each of us shared the core values of our own company. They were almost an exact match. Because we agreed on the principles, it was easy to tweak the wording and align them in priority order. Our core values and their why are at the heart of everything we do. We will describe them as a way to help you see how essential it is for the behaviors in your organization to match your core values. As you read, think how we would approach conversations with you about our core values.

> Our core values and their why are at the heart of everything we do.

A Passion for Helping Others.

The first core value is a passion for helping others. A core value should affect all aspects of your life. It's not just how you behave at work; it's how you behave everywhere. Whatever we do, our goal is to help someone else, and the money or the reward will follow later. We had someone who wanted to join the company a couple of years ago, and we asked him, "What kind of volunteer work do you do?" And he answered, "My wife makes me go serve soup at the soup kitchen." Then we said, "Tell me about a pro bono work you've done." He answered, "I found out a long time ago that if you don't charge a client something for it, they won't see value in it, and they won't work as hard."

We look at it as, "Are you really passionate about helping

others, and is it part of who you are?" We have a lot of people that we help on the side. It's only going to take a couple of hours here and there to help, so why not help? That person will remember and one day, somewhere in the future, she'll recommend you to someone else.

One thing that comes to mind is paying it forward. We look at the people who have helped us and continue to help us. They do it because they care and because they have compassion. They do it out of a servant's heart. It inspires us to do the same for others, and to pay it forward.

The idea of a servant heart strikes a chord because we have both studied servant leadership from Robert Greenleaf. At the end of the day, the best gift we can give to someone is ourselves, to serve them and help them succeed or win, or to support and encourage them.

If we're going to be a servant leader, it can't be something that is faked or forced. It has to be from a genuine place. This requires us to look deeper and ask, "Is this really part of my DNA? Do I really believe this to be true? In my core purpose, do I really understand that part of my life is to give it away, and it's all about serving others?"

The first step in a leadership transformation, which we'll delve into more deeply in chapter five, is self-awareness. You have to understand where you are. It is amazing how often we get into a conversation with a leader who has little or no self-awareness.

We were coaching a CEO and executive team, and they had a really clear-headed, driven CEO who owns, along with some investors, the company he's worked for a number of years. The company was owned by a large conglomerate, and they had a lot of funding behind them. They decided to buy the company out. They then found themselves in the situation of ownership.

Ownership changes things. The CEO has a head of engineering on his team who he has worked with for sixteen years, but now the dynamics of how they work together is different. He needs the HoE (head of engineering) to step up to the plate and change some behaviors. But he was resistant. Through individual coaching, we uncovered the root problem.

How?

We asked the HoE for his story. "I worked for him for three years and gave up a bunch of my family life and work life so that I could do this for him."

We started talking about self-awareness and asked him, "Are you aware you used the words 'I did this for [him]'?"

"Yeah, I did it for him."

We asked, "What's your motivation to do that? How did this happen?"

He said, "Well, the truth is, I'm mad that he didn't recognize what I did."

In response, we said, "So you made decisions that he didn't recognize, and now you are making him pay for it sixteen years later?"

He left that day saying, "I've really got to take a look at this, don't I?"

The baggage that he had been carrying was affecting him subconsciously and affecting the relationship between the two of them. The CEO hadn't changed. He had been himself all along. He never asked his HoE to give up his family life.

Through creating some self-awareness, we've given space and created an opportunity to have a deeper conversation on how we help create change. The truth is, if he doesn't step up his game in the company, he's going to be gone.

Now that they own the company and they don't have the huge backing that they had, everyone's got to perform. It doesn't matter what resentment he holds against the CEO, because he is being held accountable for his behavior and performance. If he is going to be able to learn and grow, he needs to be able to get out of his own way. We believe this touches on a passion for helping others.

Human Sponge

Consider the analogy of a sponge in a bucket of water. You can take the sponge, dip it in the water, squeeze it, and really fill it up with water. Pull it out, and maybe the sponge is dripping a little. If you squeeze the sponge a little bit, a little bit of water comes out. If you squeeze it a lot, a lot of water comes out.

Human sponge is really how we look at learning. We have to be human sponges. We believe you can learn something every single day. Some firms/consultants have such a set process, they squeeze the sponge and they get everything every single time, and everyone gets exactly the same treatment.

Think about it this way: The client will determine how much they will squeeze the sponge. We will bring to them everything that we've learned, but we've got a process, and we don't necessarily work with every client the same way. It's about the client's needs.

Say you've got a tool box. In your tool box you've got a hammer, pliers, screwdrivers, and a bunch of others. Not every job requires a hammer. Do you try to use that on every job first?

Would you use a hammer to buff the wax on a car?

Human sponge is about what we give back to our clients. The deeper part of it is that we are always absorbing. We believe something can be learned from every single person we are around every day. The day you stop learning is the day that you die.

Anytime a client comes to us seeking our help, we ask, "What business books have you read in the last year?" The wrong response is, "I've gotta tell you. I've run a bunch of companies, I've learned all this stuff, and it's my turn to give back. There's really nothing anyone can teach me at this phase because I've done it all." That completely flies in the face of human sponge.

A fact about a sponge is that in order for it to be efficient and effective, it actually has to be wet in order to absorb.

From our perspective, we don't believe we're in a teaching environment. We believe we create learning environments. One of the worst things a teacher can do is think they are simply dumping information. The reality is we don't teach people anything, we help them learn. When they learn, they get it, and can implement it, and change their lives, thoughts, beliefs, and patterns.

At the end of the day, human sponge means: Am I wet enough to learn? Am I in the mix with them saying, "I'm not the teacher, I'm learning with you?"

We might have something to offer or you might have something, but these things can be sponged together.

It means asking yourself, "Am I open? Am I open to hear? Am I open to transformation? Am I open to having an idea rejected or challenged? Am I even open to encouragement or receiving a compliment?"

A human sponge is going to be open to whatever life has to offer.

Synterdependence

Synterdependence is the combination of three concepts:

1) Synergy

2) Interdependence

3) Independence

Simply put, this gets to how we operate with others. There is a certain level of independence required that allows accountability and other things to come into play. You and the people on your team have to be able to take ownership. You have to be able to go and do the work. We're not going to hold hands and drive/manage them. There is an expectation that people will go and do what they need to do in order to survive/grow.

And yet, there is also the recognition that we cannot be experts in everything. Even within our system, different people have varying levels of expertise. We aren't trying to create a Jack-of-all-trades. We want to know who the experts are in different areas. Knowing who those people are means we have to be willing to hand things off to those people, and trust they have the capability to get it done. That is the interdependency. Interdependence has to be allowed to come into play.

Now comes synergy. If we are both independent and interdependent, it allows for a space where we can come together and talk, think, and brainstorm in a way where the synergy can expand.

Altogether synterdependence means you are self-account-able, you aren't trying to be all things to all people. You value the power of working within a group. There is an underlying concept that the ego is not getting in the way. It's hard to have energy if you think you are the expert in the room. You can't have interdependence this way.

These three things have to be balanced in such a way that they can balance on the "tip of a pin."

In any team or company, you need your people to be 100 percent themselves, 100 percent of who they are emotionally, relationally, spiritually, etc., because that is what they have to bring to the table. In the same way, you need to be 100 per-cent you in the same way. With that in mind, there is a bit of autonomy that happens. When two autonomous people come together 100 percent engaged, there is an amazing interde-pendence that can occur that then creates synergy.

Intense Intentionality

We are very clear and intentional about all of our relation-ships. At no point do we ever claim to own the truth. There could be several owners of the truth in any given situation; it's a matter of perspective. Some consultants are so concerned with keeping their job with a CEO that they will "bow."

In the past, we received a referral to work with the head of a real estate investment trust (REIT). The owner called his company a "billion dollar company." The truth is, it's a billion dollar REIT. Their revenue is not a billion dollars. He's trying to sell that, so we should have already seen there was a core values issue. The actual revenue of the company is somewhere around $20,000,000 to $25,000,000.

The owner wanted help with training his people and creating leaders. As we got down the path, it became clear he had no self-awareness, plus he wanted to tell us how to train his people. We said, "No. We were referred to you because you needed something that we have. We aren't going to do your training with your people. You can do that. Don't waste your money with us."

He got upset and big-chested and said, "Do you know how many people I'm connected with? Do you know how many leads I can generate for you?"

We said, "No, and it doesn't really matter."

He said, "I'm interested in what you have. Would you put together a proposal for me?"

We walked out of there knowing this guy was going to be nothing but trouble.

Sometimes we need to know when to walk away.

We put together a normal proposal. And he said, "This is too high."

Stand your ground. "Well, this is our rate."

"I've got so many others who are bidding for this who are half the price."

"Go for it," we said.

All too often, even in a sales scenario, we are afraid to say no. You want to find some way to provide a service to these people. There will always be others who are willing to get into a bidding war to get a job, but we aren't. We weren't rude about it, but there was never a point that we would have pulled a punch. It was both intentional and intense.

There's an old saying. "The truth will set you free..." But the second part of that is, "But it might piss you off first."

There are a couple of other familiar philosophies that have guided us: "A quiet no is as good as a loud one." and "Kill 'em with kindness, but kill 'em."

It isn't about being rude. You don't have to be rude, but it is about sharing a truth. Sometimes people don't take that truth the same way. One of the people that comes to mind on this is Simon Cowell. Think about all the criticism he took. The only times he got rude was when people pushed back on him. Ultimately, he was concise and clear, and it was what people really needed to know. They did not have the talent to make it; probably, 1 percent of people make it into entertainment. It's such a small, small number, so why waste time.

When you picture the word "intense," the picture might be an in-your-face MMA wrestler who's going to let you have it. If you think about the word, it's really about an expressive zeal, energy, concentration, or passion. Popular TED Talks speaker and author Angela Duckworth calls it, "Grit—[it's] about working on something you care about so much that you're willing to stay loyal to it…it's doing what you love, but not just falling in love—staying in love." (Grit)

We don't claim to own the truth, but when asked, we're going to give it.

When the truth gets hidden:

We believe that one of Nexecute's greatest assets is the Yin and Yang that stems from our individual stories that we live out in the current reality. The principle of Yin and Yang is that two opposites attract and complement each other. Neither pole is superior to the other as they strive to reflect a correct balance to achieve harmony. As much as humanly possible, this is the goal of our partnership and the way we seek to operate. Each of us pursues truth with abandon. It won't surprise you that it comes from our individual story.

BUILDING UPON CORE VALUES

As an organization grows, it's natural for those core values and traits that were once so clear to start to become murky. This is inevitable because an organization typically doesn't grow overnight. You add more team members as needed, identifying capacity and growth in a way that's smart for the company. Adding team members at a moderate rate will give you a strange period in which you have new members of a small team that will start to instill their own values into the organization, rather than simply adopting the original ones. In a smaller group, this is bound to happen. What's important in this phase is to clearly begin to establish (or perhaps redefine) those core values.

> As an organization grows, it's natural for those core values and traits that were once so clear to start to become murky.

How Do You Find Your Core Values?

We suggest that they are discovered. You may already be demonstrating them on a daily basis but just not communicating them. In this stage of the game, it is essential to focus on your core competency and what you authentically desire to deliver. Core values will drive and sync with organizational goals.

During this period, it's essential to take time for internal meetings about the alignment and vision of the organization. Of course, you should be working on a strategic plan for growth, but it's just as important to be focusing and establishing the culture. To do this, it's helpful to go through discussions of each leader's core values.

At Nexecute®, we have special exercises and conversations designed to help our clients and partners discover their own core values. These exercises allow open and easy communication in a way that is both fun and engaging.

In order to discover your own core values, you can start the discovery process by gathering your team and asking a set of discovery questions.

During this conversation, consider asking each other these questions:

- *When first creating this organization, what did we set out to achieve?*
- *How are we doing/how is our progress?*
- *How do you think we got there?*
- *Based on our conversation from number three, what key values brought us here?*

These questions will bring forth conversations that will inevitably discuss people's core values and in so doing, find what's important to them and how their culture should reflect this.

Let's look at an example. Using a totally made-up organization, let's answer some of these questions so you can see what we mean by discussing core values.

When first creating this organization, what did we set out to achieve? We set out to become the Great Lakes' number one T-shirt graphics manufacturer for small- to medium-sized businesses and nonprofit organizations.

Where are we on that path? We are the leader in Michigan and Ohio T-shirt apparel, but have not broken into the New York, Wisconsin, Indiana, and Illinois markets.

How do you think we got there? By providing quick turn-around on tight deadlines, with accuracy and attention to detail on the graphics provided to us by clients. By striving to optimize production by listening internally to team members and refining our sales process based off that feed-back. By creating a fun environment with team members that want to help grow the company.

Based on our conversation from number three, what key values brought us here? Speed, accuracy, open communication, and fun. We guide leaders through this extensive process.

Hopefully this will give you an idea of the conversations on discovering those core values that have brought your organization to its current status, and that will help propel your organization to reach its goals. While core values don't create culture, and people's behaviors do, it's still incredibly important to figure out what they are, as they will ultimately influence one another in innumerable ways with huge impacts on the organization overall. Now, what do we do with this?

A company must have the discipline to ensure that all hiring practices and procedures are ensuring we are hiring people who have our core values. We also need to ensure that as we discover people who are misaligned to the core values, they are eliminated.

Every organization is made up of process and people. Every culture problem is a problem with process or people. Are you self-aware enough to understand which one you need to address? It's important for leaders to engage every member of the core leadership team in this discussion.

Make no mistake, this takes vulnerability. We agree with Dr. Brené Brown (author of *Daring Greatly*) that vulnerability does not mean being weak. Arguably, vulnerability is the greatest measure of strength. Vulnerability means a willingness to be wrong, a willingness to be seen as imperfect, a willingness to ask questions, and a willingness to say, "I don't know!" and get the opinions of others.

> *"It's not about being the best in the world,*
> *it's about being the best* for *the world."*
> —DEWITT JONES, PHOTOGRAPHER FOR
> *NATIONAL GEOGRAPHIC.*

We are all about the truth and helping people understand that whatever is in the darkness has more power than that which is in the light, so let's get into the light so we can deal with it.

The first step in getting to the truth is to listen.

There is so much joy in mentoring younger people who have a desire to coach others. They may be personal coaches, executive coaches, life coaches, or transformational coaches. One of them asked to shadow us during one of our sessions with a team. The focus of the work with this team was building team cohesion through working on trust. She watched attentively for the entire session and afterwards we asked, "So what did you think about today's session?" And she said,

"I can't believe how little you said. But what you said was so powerful."

That's the lesson to learn. The key is to listen, listen, listen. Then when asked, you can give the truth.

How do you speak the truth? Clearly and with kindness.

In one of our sessions with a senior leadership team, they were discussing the challenge of working with one of their customers and not meeting the agreed upon deadlines with the customer. Teammates were engaged and sharing their honest opinions on how to move forward with the customer. After thirty minutes, the general manager blurted, "We don't tell the customer the truth!" The brows of everyone tightened, chairs were pushed back from the table, and a few of the team members dropped the pens in their hands. You could see the disgust.

In a private meeting with him afterwards, we said to him, "We have something to talk to you about, and it's not easy, but we want you to hear us clearly. You said to your leadership team, 'We don't tell the client the truth.'"

And he said, "Well, I didn't tell them to lie."

We said, "You said, 'We don't tell the client the truth.' That is lying. And quite frankly, not only is it lying, it doesn't match with your company's core value, which is 'truth and integrity in all relationships.' You're going to have to face that, because this isn't the way a leader operates."

That's unfiltered, it's naked, it's passionate, but it's the truth.

Life Is a Journey

How we approach life is determined by our mindset. It's quite easy to become totally focused on a specific goal. And then what? Dan Sullivan, founder of Strategic Coach and author of *Learning How to Avoid the Gap*, teaches the concept of "the gap." It's the gap between where we are today and where we want to be. The problem is that people live in the gap because there is always going to be a gap between our ideals and where we are. We get so focused on a specific goal that we forget about the path.

For us, life truly is a journey. Not every day is a great day. But what can we learn from that day? How do we take it forward, and learn from it? Do we use it to positively affect where we are going? How do we have fun with it? After all, the journey ends exactly the same way. Therefore, we get to determine the kinds of things we want to have left behind. What kind of life do we want to have had? There are going to be trials and tribulations, but do we really want to surround ourselves with people who are not aligned with our core values? Do we really want to set goals that are unrealistic? Do we really want to become so materialistic that it becomes about the things, and we lose sight of what is really important? And that's what each and every day can bring. And know that every day is a bit of a reset.

As we have stated, we believe every person's story matters, and that your story tells who you are, what you are up against, and how you face the world.

We believe it is essential for leaders to become students of their story. In fact, whenever we start working with a new team, we ask everyone to share their story. Depending on the size of the team, we ask that they take twenty to thirty minutes to do so. After the initial shock, the color returns to their faces and most have this quizzical look as if to ask, "You can't be serious." We are.

We've come to realize that most people, including us, were never taught that your story really matters and that knowing your story, owning it, and sharing it in an appropriate setting with the appropriate people is healthy. For teams, it is the foundation of building cohesion and ultimately, trust. We let them know that we are not asking for intimate details of their story. Rather we invite them to share pertinent parts of their story that will help people learn more about them and connect with them, from where they grew up, their childhood, and what got them to this place in their life, personally and professionally.

Mind you, the process takes time—often hours. We start by modeling for them how to tell their story and in doing so, we are vulnerable about who we are. After hearing our story, their apprehension lessens and after a deep breath, each one begins to share. Sometimes they stammer, other times there are long pauses, and in a number of instances, tears well up in their eyes as they speak of heartache, loss, disappointments, setbacks, etc. People connect with the pain of others. After all, it's a common denominator of life. There is almost something sacred about the moment. People are humanized and connection deepens.

It's good for people to hear our stories. They are completely different and yet serendipitously we end up in the same space, teaching the same principles.

We both ended up in our family business. Chris chose the family business of running a restaurant chain and food manufacturing operation and Mark the family business of public ministry. Both of us were driven by something to prove, in some way hoping to prove to others that we were worthy of our positions and roles in our jobs. Neither of us knew the importance of owning our story or being aware of the things that drove us or in our worse moments, triggered us. Given our personalities, we powered through situations with our intellect, grit, and determination. We both knew the importance of building teams and that others were important to our collective success. At the same time, we were not aware of how other people experienced us. Truth be told, it wasn't always pleasant. We enjoy people. It's just that we were often the source of rubs in relationships.

We both knew that too many times, our forceful reactions were triggered by something but didn't have the courage or skills to explore what was behind them. It wasn't until after we made career changes that we had to embark on a journey into our inner world. We had spent much of our life focusing on WHAT we did. It was time to start working on WHO we are.

Today, in team settings, we speak honestly about our stories and we conclude our time with a variation of these words, "Our story is our story. It matters ... every chapter, every disappointment, and every victory. And, no matter what, we get to write the next chapter."

This is why knowing the "gap" matters. There will be times when we fail, when we make choices that we regret, or have heavier consequences. The choice now is what we will do next. We get to write the next chapter. We are learning that our choice matters.

Enough research has been done to show that successful

people are people who choose to be positive. Shawn Achor writes, "Focusing on the good isn't just about overcoming our inner grump to see the glass half full. It's about opening our minds to the ideas and opportunities that will help us be more productive, effective, and successful at work and in life." (*The Happiness Advantage*)

To teach this to our clients, we use a tool called "The Accountability Ladder." It addresses what you do in the moment that something happens. Something happens, and it will trigger a series of events, and you have a choice in that moment: do you go down the ladder, or do you go up the ladder?

Going down the ladder is a descent to the victim mentality. You get into all the problems of why something can't work, the blame game, and/or excuses. In these negative types of behavior, you don't look toward a resolution. These tend to be unconscious behaviors. People have learned these habits throughout life, and in some cases, it's a coping mechanism.

One thing we know is that the human mind is wired for negative bias. When something happens, we go into our most natural state and use our defense mechanisms, which can often be "Oh, woe is me. This is someone else's fault, and this is why they've done it to us."

The change is that the conscious behavior needs to make the choice to go up the ladder, where you still acknowledge what happened and say, "Yes, this happened and it sucks, but what am I going to do about it? What's the solution? Where am I going to take this forward?" It starts with being curious.

As we think in terms of becoming accountable, which is a very conscious step to do so, it allows us to have a different level of transformation. This begs the question of are we truly being accountable in our own lives?

Unfortunately, many people choose to wallow in self-pity. They focus on all the problems, and that is such a depressing place to be. As advisors, we want to inspire people to see the choice that they have in each moment. Ernest Hemingway wrote, "Today is only one day in all the days that will ever be. But what will happen in all the other days that ever come can depend on what you do today."

When we ask, "How are you?" and someone starts complaining, we often say, "That is a really terrible situation. What are you doing to change that?" And sometimes, what you are doing is getting them into solution mode. They are unaware that they are going down this ladder, but you can give them something that helps turn them around. Once you've done that a few times, then when you ask, "How are you?" they already know what's coming and they are already thinking about solutions, instead of just wallowing in self-pity.

Your company's core values could be similar to ours or uniquely your own. What matters is this: they need to be specific to your company. You need to believe in them passionately and faithfully live by them. Practically, you need to be able to hold people accountable to—including hiring and firing—your core values.

Removing Toxic People

Sometimes we will coach a client to remove someone from a team. Their contribution doesn't outweigh the detriment, and we will suggest they either be removed or perhaps their future needs to be freed up. On many occasions, we have heard a senior executive say, "We finally took that person off the team, and it's like a weight lifted off our shoulders. The team's performance completely turned around. The culture has turned around. You both were right. We should have done that a long time ago."

When someone is not aligned with the core values, the impact is toxic—sometimes high levels of toxicity, sometimes low. Either way, it's toxic and is pervasive. We don't exactly know why it takes leaders so long to make this decision. We simply ask leaders to hone their skills at noticing the obvious and subtle core value misalignment. And as they notice, we encourage them to be courageous and make the tough call. We know that every time the person is gone, they say to us, "Why didn't we do this a long time ago?"

> We finally took that person off the team, and it's like a weight lifted off our shoulders.

As we started working with another client, they had just parted ways with the CEO. We knew that there was a core value mismatch that was having quite an impact throughout the organization. What's interesting is what happened next. When the CEO left, the CEO's personal assistant, who seemed like an A-player, also took a job at a different organization. After they hired a new personal assistant, they discovered that there was only enough work for a half-time position, not a full-time position. The organization was aware of work that they thought was getting done, just wasn't, and it became painfully obvious that the former personal assistant was a C-player who was hiding in plain site. This was a scenario where she had nearly everybody fooled. She had the core values of the company, but she just wasn't performing as an A-player.

As we work so closely with organizations, it often becomes clear that one or more of the team members need individual coaching. The premise is that we need to see what is motivating a person to behave the way they do in a work setting where they are having a negative impact. Out of the gate, we assess the obstacles the person may be facing and then determine the specific steps or tools in the need for self-awareness and self-management. The outcome's objectives are clear. We want the coachee to:

1. Embrace and integrate the ongoing process of personal development, engaging in self-assessment and self-management.

2. Learn and integrate the skill sets (dynamics) of transformational leadership.

3. Be equipped with the tools to calibrate his/her personal life according to their unique purpose, values, and strengths, concluding with a concise purpose statement and mission statement.

What kind of obstacles does our process uncover? Here are some examples.

One woman spent the day with us in an introductory session. She shared her story and how committed she was to her long-time boss, taking on many projects behind the scenes with little or no credit. As the organization grew and new team members were added, it turns out the more senior leaders were added to the team, thereby narrowing her scope of influence.

What was rising in her was resentment toward her boss and the belief that her boss didn't appreciate her or recognize her value to the team. This perceived belief was causing conflict with her boss and her teammates. It took hours to uncover this obstacle. When she finally had the aha moment, she was relieved and embarrassed. No wonder Robert E. Quinn wrote, "When people alter their interior world they also alter their exterior world." (*Building the Bridge as You Walk on It*)

The obstacles we face come regardless of gender, age, or level of education. For instance, one of our coachees was John, a team leader who was continually bumping heads with another gifted member of his team, Stephen. The senior leadership didn't want to lose either of these gifted men, as they were working on cutting-edge processes. From the moment we started working with John, he was receptive. He willingly shared his story and we uncovered a few obstacles that had been following him his entire career. He was ready to make the change. However, he had burned so many bridges with Stephen because of past ways of relating that Stephen was exasperated with John and was ready to find another job at a different organization.

Because we had witnessed firsthand John's commitment to self-management, we knew that he was willing to change his pattern of relating with Stephen. In fact, we were preparing for the time in the not-so-distant future with John when we would mediate a conversation between the two of them. Stephen beat us to the punch when he, unsolicited, set up a meeting with John. We encouraged John to listen, truly listen for the real issues.

The day arrived for the meeting. John blocked out three

hours in his calendar as an olive branch and to show his willingness to listen. He outlined the issue between the two of them in just two minutes and then proceeded to listen. Instead of this meeting opening up the lines of communication for making amends, John's outline was met with silence. Stephen didn't say a word. The contentious relationship was becoming more awkward by the second. After minutes, John broke the silence and as humbly as he could said, "I am willing to learn, Stephen. I am willing to listen." He paused, cleared his throat, and asked Stephen some questions. Stephen opened up as John listened. After three hours, the men stood up and gave each other a hug. Barriers were broken, and they became vulnerable. The end result was they began to work more collaboratively and had a greater impact on the bottom line.

Good people, smart people, well-meaning people sometimes need help from the outside to help them unpack the obstacles or uncover the blind spots. This type of clarity leads to personal and professional success.

We have been introduced to brilliant people in the business world, some of which are like Sheldon from *The Big Bang Theory*. They are very intelligent but with a low EQ. They have good intent and are driven to do the right thing, but they leave dead bodies in their path. Stephen could have easily become one of those dead bodies, even though he was essential to the forward success of the organization.

Both of these guys were aligned with the core values, so this wasn't an issue of core values. This was a personality clash issue. Even A-players that line up perfectly with the core values may run into problems with team members. It is a human issue, and if you dedicate the time to helping conflicted team members find clarity together, you can create huge success and growth.

In all aspects of change within an organization, you have to be willing to be honest. No one can come into a company with a plan to help implement change and create clarity if you hide your problems under the bed.

One CEO we've been working with had been really honest and clear about the results. He had all the things we would want to see in a CEO. And yet, there was almost always someone on the team who had trouble coming around, and not taking ownership, etc. The easiest path in this case would be to terminate them, to step back and say that this just isn't working out and the company is moving in a different direction that is growing beyond his capabilities and maybe it's time for someone else. So why keep him? The guy had the core values of the company and that is sometimes one of the hardest things to find in someone. It was time to make a decision about how to move forward.

When we got to talking about what the real issues were (of leadership, management, etc.), we decided that we would provide individual coaching, giving the guy a shot. The key with coaching is to face reality, to be honest about where a person is today and where they need to be tomorrow or the next day, and walking the path together to try to close that gap.

It is amazing, though, how often we uncover other things that are going on. Blocks. Impediments.

Years ago, Brené Brown burst into our consciousness and started a conversation on vulnerability movement with her initial TEDx Houston Talk. Millions (over 40,000,000 as of this writing) are viewing her other talks and reading her books, looking to her as the expert on shame and vulnerability. One of the keys to vulnerability that we've been using and that she talks about is the role of "story." Virtually every individual coaching session in the Recalibrate YouTM process begins with us asking our client to share with us their story. First, we have them diagram each decade on a large easel pad. Then we ask them to tell their story decade by decade. What comes to light are "themes" that are part of their story because story tells you who you are, where you came from, and what you are up against.

This is usually a two- to four-hour process where we pause and say things like, "Wait a minute, you've been like this since you were a kid." For them it is: "You will do the best you can. Nobody will outwork you. And you need recognition of this. So when you don't get that, you feel like you aren't wanted and needed, and it's been like this since you were a little kid. Do you see how that happens even today as a fifty-one-year-old man?"

"Oh, yeah, I do."

"Okay, we've got to deal with that."

It's all a process but at the end of the day, a very human one. Everyone has a story and knowing your team's story will be an important part of knowing your company.

Next Steps

Knowing how to move a company forward isn't an exact science. It's never the same twice. Part of what is great about our situation, but also a bit of an Achilles heel, is that a lot of times when we go in to work with a client for the first time, they are "sold" before we even walk through the door. But we don't really even know what we are going in for.

As an example, we once flew to Boston for a couple of meetings and had a client there who said to us, "You've got to meet this guy, he really needs your help. I've told them all about you and about what you can do and he's really interested." We were going in not even knowing what the problem was or anything about the situation.

We named the process, The Elephant Conversation™. It is when we come in and our whole goal is to understand what's really the underlying issue within the room and/or within the team.

That begins with saying "Let's have a conversation, CEO to CEO. Let's talk about what's working and what's not working for you. What creates frustration? What are some things that you believe are a real danger to success? Who's on your team? Now tell me a little about your team."

And then at that point we'll say, "Let me share with you a framework that we utilize." This is based on "Top Grading." What makes an A-, B-, or C-player? And then we'll challenge them to grade their team members. Depending on what they flag on their team, we're going to see if they have any people who are questionable.

Or if they have all A-players on their team, we're going to question them further because that never happens. It's not a reality. Then we get into the areas that are functioning well and those that aren't. Where are the disputes in the team? Who are the better performers? We are able to show them that they don't have all A-players on their team. What are the core values of your organization?

The whole idea is to turn them on to issues within their organization that they are ignoring, they don't recognize, or maybe that they do recognize but don't know how to address. The direction of the conversation stems from the first couple of questions, which are centered around, "What are you excited about?", "What's frustrating you or holding you back?", and "Why are we here, and why do you want to talk to us? What is the problem you are looking to solve?"

Sometimes those conversations last ten minutes, and those don't usually become clients. Or they can go several hours, sometimes multiple calls, and those turn out to be the best clients.

It's tailored. You're taking the time to get to know them and why they need our help.

We never walk into a session with the intent to sell anything. We don't consider that we have anything to "sell." Our goal is "Let's understand the problem and let's talk." Maybe there is a way we can help you, and maybe there isn't. Maybe we are the right ones to help or maybe there is someone else. If it's someone else or some other process, we'll refer you to the right place. It's about your success. If we can be the ones to help you, we'll be very happy to do so, because that fulfills our first core value.

We Are Not a Fit for Everyone.

One of our clients referred us to a guy who runs a large law firm and said they could use our help. We told them about our process and the firm was excited about it. We flew in to ask him the same sort of questions, and after about one and a half hours at the end of the session and talking about goals and making everything work he said, "This is really great. When do we start?"

We looked him back in the eye and said, "Well, we have to tell you. We're not the right group for you. We spent time really understanding your problem and we could probably help you with this or that, but quite frankly, you need someone who specializes in law practices, because some of your issues are very specific." And we gave him the name of somebody else. We sat there and he was looking off and we asked him, "Tell me, what's going on in your mind right now?" He said, "I kind of feel like I just got dumped at the prom."

It struck us as funny.

After that, we actually became good friends.

That's just the way that it went. What we had at the time was not appropriate for what he was looking for. And that will happen probably one out of five or six conversations we have with people on a prospect list.

Integrity in business is looking at a client, knowing they would cut you a check, but knowing it's not the right fit for anyone. The ability to say "no" in business can be a positive thing, though most people view it as a negative. You shouldn't be willing to sell something they can't use.

In everything we do, we want to make sure there is a clear path moving forward, and we have to ask a lot of questions in order to do that. Sometimes we have people refer us to someone saying, "You need Nexecute," and they come to us saying, "So-and-so says I need you."

And we ask them, "Well, what is your goal?"

They say, "I want to build a team."

"Great, that's what we do. Our job is to help you build a

cohesive leadership team and here's our process. Are you interested?"

"Absolutely. Can we start next week?"

In this case, thirty minutes later and we were done.

CHAPTER 4

"Problems don't seem to just go away, so you must deal with them quickly and decisively. At the end of the day, you have to be able to look at yourself in the mirror and have the courage to make the tough decisions. Then, live with them."

-MICHAEL KIRCHNER, PRESIDENT

The Courageous Leader

What is a leader?

This is a question that has been asked for ages of human history, and yet there is often a lack of clarity about it. Ask any number of people this question and you'll get a wide range of definitions.

Each one of us has seen examples of a variety of leaders throughout our careers, but the definition of true leadership has been the subject of great debate. Some define leadership in terms of quietness versus charisma, while others use color theory to define leadership styles. Regardless of what you may think, one thing is certain: Leaders who can transform cultures and successfully achieve results are going to lead people to win. The very best leaders ignite transformation and create results. Their core values will drive their behaviors and they will never waiver. They are relentless in the pursuit of their vision and share that vision in a manner that excites others, inspiring them to follow. This can only be done with a commitment to building leadership skills and ongoing communication.

These are highly developed skills that need to be perpetually honed and kept sharp. This requires a great amount of self-awareness and willingness to improve. Great leaders always feel that they can get better. We view these people as transformational leaders.

TRANSFORMATIONAL LEADERS

The "transformation" adjective is of utmost importance. Transformational leaders know that to offer their best to the organization, they need to be aware of what it takes to "morph" with the people and circumstances around them, not control them. This means moving from a rigid state to a state that is grounded, and being self-aware of both what is going on in their head and what is happening in their heart. That's why we believe that transformational leaders are courageous. The very word "courage" has it roots, not in being heroic, but being able to tell the story from your heart. Courageous leaders are willing to spend their life learning to live and lead from both their head and their heart.

As we mentioned, one of our core values is a passion for helping others, and this passion drives everything we do and how we do it. Another core value is continuous, lifelong learning, which means that when we go inside an organization, we want to teach and help execute; however, we also want to learn from everyone around us. We understand that self-improvement never stops and that defining what leadership is will be important for the organization as a whole.

What does leadership mean to you? The best leaders have figured out the difference between management and leadership, but this isn't always an easy task. If you Google "modern leaders," you will see individuals who have accomplished enough to be noticed by the media. Some are so famous that you know them by one word: Oprah, Gates, Buffett, Musk, Zuckerberg, or Bezos. Study leadership throughout history and you will read about Nelson Mandela, John Rockefeller, Gandhi, or Alexander the Great. Is every person who achieves, invents, or accomplishes big things a leader? What makes a leader?

> If a person commands every decision, that person is not a leader.

Often, many of the examples we see in the media are not leaders in the true sense of the word, but truly great managers. The truth is, redefining leadership inside your organization is important. If a person commands every decision, that person is not a leader. They are acting like a manager. If a person continually focuses on the minutia, that person is not a leader. They are acting like a manager.

Managers often don't trust their people as much as leaders do. They simply want the task done and completed. Period. They want to control things; however, by doing so, it keeps the thinking and decision making to themselves. It's really not about empowering people, but accomplishing tasks. A leader endeavors to empower others to think and take action without their direct input.

What's your leadership culture?

THE DIFFERENCE BETWEEN LEADERS AND MANAGERS
Business Leaders Versus Managers

Often the words "leaders" and "managers" are considered interchangeable, or, at the very least, their responsibilities are sometimes confused. While many in the business world believe the two roles to be roughly the same, we take a different, more distinctive approach by defining their unique differences and how each one impacts results. Business leaders and managers occupy different roles, to say the least.

Defining Leaders and Managers

At the outset, we want to clarify that we see "leader" and "manager" as modes of thinking, instead of a role, description, or title. One is not more important than another. Both are essential in achieving world-class results. A role description may well determine the amount of time an individual will spend in either mode. Leaders and managers are both needed, but it's important to understand their unique roles.

In a leadership mode of thinking, one is responsible for and is measured by the results that are achieved. In a manager mode of thinking, one is responsible for assuring tasks are completed and processes followed. Again, a role in the organization will determine the amount of time and energy spent in each mindset or mode. For instance, a person in a senior leadership position would spend more time in leader mode, whereas someone in charge of a smaller team or group would spend more time in manager mode.

As we flesh this out further, think in terms of the "mindset" of each:

In Leadership Mode ... You Innovate

A leader is always looking for ways to achieve the bigger picture—executing the vision. Envision a conductor of an orchestra. A conductor is responsible for the overall performance: keeping everyone together, ensuring each section of the orchestra performs their parts well, and shaping the phrasing so the music is played correctly. Likewise, a leader has the freedom to interpret and innovate, assuring that the right people are executing in the right environment, according to the right plan.

In Manager Mode ... You Elevate

While leaders innovate, managers elevate—pushing the team to strive for excellence in every operation. They drive the belief that every process is open to evaluation and every system is geared toward continuous improvement. They identify roadblocks and are keenly aware of their individual team members' strengths and weaknesses inside and out. They understand how to boost performance, heighten team effectiveness, and provide the solution to achieving the goals.

In Leadership Mode ... You Embrace Change

Leaders pull the team to achieve more. Therefore, they embrace change. It's only natural that leaders are constantly thinking of change; after all, how can things be improved if everything stays the same? It's always a risk to try something new, but leaders are willing to take risks in the hopes of something better. It may mean pulling a highly functioning team to the next level or correcting something that is dysfunctional in another team, while in leadership mode, they are always looking for new, out-of-the-box solutions. With this type of exponential thinking, they not only create change, they implement it in a variety of ways: through a new team member, a new phase, or a new strategy. Subsequently, leaders hold people accountable for the outcome.

In Manager Mode ... You Focus on Systems and Structures

Sometimes teams don't need a leader mindset. They need a manager mindset. At this point, they need someone to focus on the systems and structures in play to be able to meet those set goals. Understanding the steps and rules within a system is critical for a manager. If they know the process and how the team carries out that process, they are able to account for problems that arise. Additionally, by focusing on the structure within their team, they can accurately regulate and direct all facets of the project from kickoff to evaluation, holding people accountable for specific tasks.

In Leadership Mode ... You Inspire

Leaders also pull the team by inspiring them. They invigorate them to execute the vision by over-communicating the reason–WHY–it is worth working harder, taking more risks, and achieving more than they might imagine. Leaders listen to team members and encourage those that have new ideas and different views. Inspiration is not achieved by just saying encouraging words to team members. It takes an open environment, a coaching approach with plenty of helpful examples, and guidance. Along the way, a culture is built and teams become stronger.

In Manager Mode ... You Maintain and Administer

One of the most important things a manager does is properly maintain all processes within their respective teams. In manager mode, they control and administer, allowing the organization to run at full capacity, efficiently and effectively.

It's Skill Combined with the "Art" of Being a Leader and Manager

Put simply, for an organization to achieve the desired results, managers ensure everything runs smoothly so that leaders can focus on innovation and growth. Regardless of title, key influencers know that each mode is unique and critical. We've simply introduced some of the skills for each mode.

It takes awareness and intentionality for every person to practice the "art" of when it is appropriate to be a leader or manager, in other words, learning how to spend the appropriate time during any given day, practicing each mode.

Leaders and managers are both needed in a business, but given your role in the organization, what percentage of your day should be in leader mode and what percentage of your day in manager mode?

DRIVING A COMPELLING AND ENGAGING VISION

True leaders don't manage through fear. They motivate through inspiration. Great leaders are courageous problem solvers. They are willing to do what it takes to engage their team toward success, often in unexpected ways.

They start with a strong desire for something—a problem to be solved or a goal to be attained. They then build a vision around it, a vision of their world after this problem is solved or they have attained their goal. For many, that is where it stops. They may share that vision, but their path to achieving it is through managing—controlling the steps to get there.

A leader, on the other hand, goes many steps beyond. They have so much energy around their vision, that it becomes compelling to others. This is the element that can lead to unexpected greatness. When a leader shares their vision with others in such a way as to cause them to want to be a part of it, they begin to help push that vision forward. They so badly want to be part of achieving that vision that they are willing to put in a great effort, sometimes with pain and sacrifice. Because transformational leaders lead with both their head and their heart, they are caring and decisive and can quickly focus a team around a culture and mission. This is the truest definition of leadership: the ability to focus followers on the execution of organizational goals.

What is a leader without followers?

Over the years, managers have gotten bad press. The pendulum has swung so far that it's almost as if leaders are good and managers are bad. But this simply isn't true. There are great managers who are highly motivated. The process of managing may not be a good fit for a company and where that company is in its evolution. What role is that manager in? There are cases where a manager is needed because they control a situation. There is a time and place for that. It isn't at the top of a large company. It is within the business where managers are programming their teams, and managing them. Leaders have followers who are there for some greater purpose, because they lead in a way that creates engagement.

Managers tell people what to do. Often they manage tasks and processes. Great leaders don't sweat the small stuff—

which are all the little things to make something happen. They also don't sweat all the barriers. They motivate individuals and teams to success and they share their vision and engage those who want to be part of it. They know that as they find followers, and then train and encourage and focus them consistently, the combined minds will be able to overcome any obstacle and move the group toward success.

A vision doesn't have to be big to be compelling. We have seen great leaders at the top of very small organizations who are focused on what some may consider a small goal or feat. The difference is how they attract and engage their people.

IT TAKES TRUE COURAGE

True courage is about recognizing your fears and overcoming them to accomplish something greater.

Let's be clear about courage. Courage doesn't mean being fearless, reckless, or blind to reality.

Not recognizing or ignoring fears is foolhardy and will often drive bad decision making. This can be very costly. We often say that to build trust, a leader must be willing to be vulnerable and this takes courage. Here, vulnerability means both acknowledging and facing one's fears. Vulnerability can also mean a willingness to be wrong, to be seen as imperfect, to ask questions, to say "I don't know," and to ask for the opinions of others.

Courage is necessary to clarify and understand the risks and push through the uncomfortable, in life and business. The status quo and comfort zones hold people back all the time. A lack of courage to take a risk and push past fears causes people to remain in a comfort zone of unfulfilled potential. Great leaders learn how to be courageous when it counts.

There is another type of courage necessary as a leader and that is the courage to trust others. We've all experienced leaders who believe they're the smartest person in the room. They micromanage every detail until they're exhausted, their team is exhausted, and everyone feels like giving up. They don't communicate confidence and courage because they don't give their employees enough room to grow and make mistakes. This type of leader is about control.

Great leaders know that if they have surrounded themselves with other core values aligned, like-minded, and driven people, they don't need to own every action. They can continue to drive the vision, knowing that others will help them get there. This allows a leader to delegate the vision's execution to others. It is the courage to let go of micromanaging the tasks that lead to the success of the vision that makes a great leader.

> Great leaders know that if they have surrounded themselves with other core values aligned, like-minded, and driven people, they don't need to own every action.

This, mind you, doesn't mean that there is no accountability; it's really quite the opposite. Leaders must also have the courage to have constant candid conversations with their people. People must always know where they stand, whether good or bad, and what needs to happen to excel. In the end, leaders must have the courage to let go of people who aren't aligned to the values and behaviors of the company or cannot achieve the results to be successful in their role.

Great leaders also have the courage to stay focused on an unwavering path, despite naysayers or what the competition is doing. You cannot react to every price cut or initiative of your competitor, critic, or even client. You must remain laser-focused on your culture and your goals to win, and it takes courage to do that.

This type of courageous leadership inspires everyone else. This type of leader has a clearly defined culture for their group and is driven to keep their culture intact. They cannot waver from their path because the consequences of wavering can be damaging to the level of respect they receive from their followers. To that end, when they find they have someone in their ranks disruptive to their group's culture, they must get that person out of their organization. Leaders are not afraid to make the tough decisions and are willing to suffer the consequences, if any, for decisions related to what they believe.

Transformational leaders have a sense of humble confidence. There is a distinction between arrogance and confidence. Great leaders are humble enough to know they don't have all the answers, so they listen. At the same time, they are confident enough to take calculated risks.

As others on the team gain confidence, a strong positive and accountable culture is developed. This allows for more creative thinking and problem solving and the development of the idea that they can do anything. Nothing is too hard, and the team can weather anything. Attitude drives positive accountable behavior, which in turn gives the vision the best possible chance of being realized.

"It's hard to be humble when you are so good" is an arrogant behavior that also isn't part of leadership. Great leaders not only find and develop great talent on their team, they give recognition. Since they are focused on their vision and typically see the vision as bigger than themselves, they are both able and willing to give credit where credit is due. They also don't often take credit for their own work. The people who work with them truly feel that they are part of something bigger than themselves.

"LEADER" IS NOT A TITLE

A person may be given a title of "leader," but that doesn't make them one. It's amazing how many managers believe their titles and call themselves leaders. Like "respect," the leadership title is earned, not bestowed. A person in a leadership position cannot demand others to give them respect or think of herself as a leader. One of our clients asked us to facilitate leadership training to second and third tier leaders in the organization. Over time most of them saw themselves as important influencers of the culture and how their influence led to overall better results. They gladly engaged in problem-solving, offered input on hiring decisions, and took action to hold their direct reports accountable. One of the leaders

> A person may be given a title of "leader" but that doesn't make them one.

114

put it this way, "When we align to our core values we're able to problem solve as a team, and more importantly listen as one. We are reminded that to function as a team words like 'they' and 'them' are eliminated from our vocabulary, and we become an 'us' and 'we'—a team."

There are certainly concepts of leadership that can be taught. Yet, while we know that people attend leadership programs all the time, it's amazing that only a small percentage not only learn the concepts, but also seem to really put them into practice. This leads us to believe that there must be something in a person's personality that will drive them to employ better leadership practices.

As we spend time addressing an organization's culture, we focus on impacting the leaders and growing them, forever. It's not just a short-term solution. We know that leaders can be taught to be better leaders when they have a willingness to learn and grow. Some really grow and become phenomenal leaders, while others go through the motions and tactics of leadership without really "getting it" and successfully putting the leadership practices into place.

Perhaps not everyone is interested in being a leader. When someone makes the choice not to be a leader, we think you should be grateful for that knowledge. We recently had an individual who is an A-player and was offered a leadership position as a promotion. They subsequently turned it down, as they didn't want the responsibility. Leadership just isn't for everyone. So, while we may not promote someone until they come forward and tell us they are ready, it is a great way to keep an A-player in their position versus promoting them and creating a C-player.

Leadership is a role and not just a set of skills. This means that it takes intentional focus to act as a leader each and every day.

Even if many—if not most—people do have the innate capability and capacity to be a leader, it doesn't mean that they will want to become one.

Those who embrace the mantle of leadership do so because it resonates with their core values. They are driven by a compulsion to forge forward because doing anything else would be contrary to their innate personalities. Leadership is a role they step into and a daily job they take seriously. Those who undertake the task do so knowingly and wouldn't have it any other way. Leaders are the courageous and transformative harbingers of evolution and revolution within a company and are responsible for enforcing its culture.

CHAPTER 5

"Learning the principles of transformation leadership moved us out of a culture of blame to one of self-awareness and personal responsibility. "

-MARK KIRCHMER, OWNER AND PARTNER

Transformational Leadership Plus Teamwork

Tricia is an active administrative assistant with a desire to accomplish tasks and bring excellence to the organization. As a mother and grandmother, she has journeyed through life long enough that she now finds herself more secure in her womanhood and in her support role. That doesn't mean that she is stuck in mindless routines. She approaches her work with a desire for excellence and intentionality. While she readily admits she has control issues, she is open to transformation and welcomes the opportunity of self-improvement.

When working with a personal coach recently, Tricia listened intentionally as he shared with her the process of transformation: "It's not about trying harder. Rather, it's about training." Hearing the words, her face betrayed her confusion. He continued, "Transformation from the inside out is about putting rhythms in your life that quiet your spirit and give clarity. Actually, it's about creating space."

Wondering if that put more pressure on her and would add to her stress, Tricia pushed back, "But that means more work, doesn't it?" The coach welcomed the question and said, "It may seem like it," pausing to let the moment sink in. "Actually, it is about being less in control and more open. When we create space for quiet reflection, we start to become mindful. We become aware of the intensity of our emotions, the quickness of our reactions, and how we carry ourselves in relation to others. It just won't happen if we don't create space."

Transforming our interior world is giving intentional effort to the areas of our life we often take for granted.

Not Everyone Wants to Transform

Joyce came to work on time and for the most part completed her tasks according to spec. She seemed willing to do a little extra and seemed to smile but everyone on the team senses there was something more. No one could put their finger on it. She offered to give up some of her hours to another employee, saying, "He needed the hours more than me." She even volunteered for behind-the-scenes jobs that others shied away from. Overall, she doesn't rock the boat and admirably earns her paycheck.

Not Everyone Wants to Transform

Yet, everyone noticed that at times she seemed distracted. Her conversations would turn to troubled family members and sick pets. The most disgruntled employees were drawn to want to work with her more than anyone else. While she never seemed to initiate gossip, she attracted it like a summer bug to light.

On a particularly challenging day at work with time-crunched deadlines looming, Joyce ignored her manager's urging to "pick up the pace." In the midst of the fray, she launched into a story with another manager about her home-life. As the deadline drew closer, her pace and mood did not rise to the challenge. She's was just "there." Another teammate, noticed her laissez-faire approach, stepped in to get the job done and complete the task. Problem averted? Not so fast.

A major piece of the component was missing when it was shipped to the client. Within minutes of arrival, the disgruntled customer contacted the front office and Joyce's manager had to face the reality. Frustrated by the low performance of his team and his lackluster approach to leadership, he invited Joyce and her teammates to a meeting. Joyce was annoyed. In some of her responses, the manager could sense a "what's the big deal" attitude. He concluded by saying, "I have to document this for upper management." Joyce was livid and her toxic attitude seeped into the room as she spewed, "This has never happened to me before!"

Two weeks later, she was still ticked off about it. Her body language was closed. Her forced smiles were twisted with cynicism and her repeated message was, "I just want my freak'n paycheck."

Because we believe in transformation, we wanted Joyce to change. Typically, when coaching individuals to be a transformational leader, our desire would be to come alongside of her and offer a safe space and processes to help her transform her life. However, we also must face reality: not everyone wants to transform. Some people would rather make the choice to be toxic than to change. Being negative is comfortable for them. Dr. Phil would say "it's working" for them.

People like Joyce won't fit into an open system where personal responsibility is encouraged and serving beyond their self-interests are valued. At the end of the day, they will not make the choice for the greater good. Does this mean they are not valued as a human being? Absolutely not. However, that does not mean that they are the right *fit* for the culture.

John C. Johnson, Ph.D., says, "Though we would like to change people what we really need to focus on is the culture of the organization." People like Joyce will play bumper cars with a healthy culture as a subconscious pastime. Dr. Johnson exposes the choice a transformational leader may indeed have to face and says, "The culture will be healthier when this type of person is removed."

HOW TO MANAGE DYSFUNCTIONAL TEAMS

Having a problem with how to manage dysfunctional teams? Believe it or not, you're not alone. This is a common problem for businesses we talk to. We do have a few tips that might help, though.

Admit You Have a Problem

You know the feeling. That oppressive feeling that sits in the office as everyone hunches over their desk, never really talking unless they have to. Worse yet, you see the disengagement and eye rolls at team meetings. To say the mood is unpleasant would be an understatement. You know that something is off with the team dynamic. And you know you should do something about it, but you just keep putting it off. You keep hoping that the whole situation will somehow course correct.

We meet many smart, successful leaders who adopt this approach with people problems. Sure, they may have a pep talk or ask HR to "have a talk" but in actuality, few face it head-on. No wonder Patrick Lencioni simply states, "Facing realities of human behavior…even the most committed executive is tempted to avoid" (*The Four Obsessions of an Extraordinary Executive*).

But here's the problem: it never pays to avoid the problem. Unless the leaders within the organization take on the challenge of addressing the issues within a dysfunctional team, the only change you'll see is your quality talent moving on to new jobs to escape a miserable work environment.

It requires courage, strong leadership, and discipline to address reality. Transformational leaders committed to leading from both their head and heart will sit down and figure out a plan for dealing with the situation. It is the only way to turn a dysfunctional team into a transformational team which is cohesive and high-performing.

Take Stock

Once you've recognized that there is a problem within your workplace and that it probably has to do with your team's dynamics, it's time to start reaching out to your team. Remember, a dysfunctional team dynamic may have many different causes and it will affect each team member in a different way. Talk to your team to get a feel for why they are struggling. Hear what they need and don't rely on your assumptions. Their answers to your questions may surprise you.

Work with Your Team

Once your team has been heard, it's time for you as the leader to do what you do best: roll up your sleeves and achieve results. The real challenge in learning how to manage dysfunctional teams is getting to know the team members. As you consider how you can help your team, it can be helpful to identify key players on your team. These people are the ones who live out the core values of the organization and who embrace the transformational change that is needed to maximize results. When these people are brought together, the group dynamic will align with your plan for the future.

Make the Hard Decisions

While highlighting and promoting key players into the right position can bring a lot of positive energy to the team dynamic, it's important to remember that not everyone on your team will be a key player. More often than not, when morale is low, there is at least one person who would thrive best in another position or maybe even within another organization. While moving someone off your team is nothing to take lightly, allowing someone with misalignment in core values or who has performance issues can drag any hard-won morale boost straight back down.

Regroup and Move Forward

Once your team has started to rebuild and navigate the new, more open dynamics, the only thing left to do is regroup and move forward. Be vigilant in ensuring your team (and you) don't fall back into old habits and don't hold onto old grudges and disgruntled feelings. As your team starts to truly become transformative and produce results, it's important to keep everyone accountable. Only then will you truly see results.

HOW TEAM DYNAMICS ARE HOLDING YOUR COMPANY BACK

When you become a leader inside an organization, there is enormous pressure for you to succeed. After all, your success translates into success for your company.

Start by investing in yourself. Consider your leadership style: fine-tune your strengths and manage your weaknesses. Bring a vision and plan for success to the company, making sure that each stage is communicated thoroughly to your team and to the company at large. Solicit feedback by checking in with your colleagues.

If you still sense that morale is low and team dynamics are not what they once were, continue investigating the deeper reasons. It could be that everyone knows what to do but somehow aren't able to execute the plan. As the leader, you must become laser-focused on holding people accountable to the right priorities that will yield the right results. Over time, you will identify the gaps in people or processes. Addressing these realities will put you back on track. People will sense that your plan is executable and will ensure that organization will stay on track.

> As the leader, you must become laser-focused on holding people accountable.

What Happened to Your Team's Cohesiveness?

This is one instance where looking within to identify the problem is not necessarily going to lead to greater insight. Instead, it's time to look at the group dynamics at play within your organization and to understand how people in the middle level of your organization can be so powerful in holding your plan back.

The Role of Team Compatibility

So how does team compatibility affect outcomes so dramatically? To better understand this, we have to do some myth busting. There are two common misconceptions that must be addressed:

1. Strategic planning is the same as strategic execution of the plan.

2. Everyone in your organization is already in their best-fit job.

The first misconception is not easy to tackle. Just because you come up with a plan doesn't mean everyone knows how to make it happen or is even on board with it. It boils down to this: planning does not equal execution. You have to put as much effort into making sure the execution happens on every level of your organization as you put into your strategic planning. It's common sense, but it often gets forgotten. Remember, just because your team knows what to do doesn't mean they know how to do it or even can do it.

The second misconception is an uncomfortable truth: not everyone who is currently on your team is the best fit for your team. When momentum stalls during a turnaround phase, the culprit can usually be found within those who didn't necessarily come up with the plan but do have a hand in how the plan is executed. If those people are not on board, you have a problem.

For starters, they can become insidious voices in meetings and around colleagues. They shut the people around them down and in doing so, shut down execution of the plan. It's at this point that you start to see morale dip. Additionally, if you are doing the work of making sure your employees know how to execute the plan, you need to make sure you are not expending precious resources on people who are more invested in seeing the plan fail than seeing it succeed.

How to Handle "Roadblock Employees"

It's time to consider how these roadblock employees fit into the larger picture of how your company will function moving forward. Will they help create transformational change or will they be a barrier for those above and below them? There are no easy answers, and it's questions like this that require courage and perseverance from a leader.

USE EMOTIONAL INTELLIGENCE TO BOOST YOUR TEAM

Stan is a solid employee. He's cheerful, does his job with attention to detail, and gets along with everyone. It came as a surprise then to see a change in attitude when the company started working on their turnaround plan. In meetings, he started shooting down people's ideas, calling them negative, and taking personal offense at their suggestions. It eventually got to the point that no one on his team wanted to offer ideas and team morale plummeted. Leadership was worried that the morale in Stan's team would infect the others in the company. What went wrong?

Transformation is hard. It requires a strong sense of vision, determination, vulnerability, and a willingness to change. All of these traits may not come naturally, but science has shown that they are strong indicators of success for top performers. Another word for these traits? Emotional intelligence.

Understanding exactly how emotional intelligence supports the transformation of a team or organization can be helpful in identifying and cultivating these traits in yourself and your team. Below, we'll break down the three traits your team should embrace in order to excel in their roles, as well as move forward with the organization.

EMBRACE CHALLENGES

The first step any organization needs to take when they are looking to change their vision is to boldly take stock of what's working and what's not. We see happening in a few different phases, all of which are part of our process, The Results Optimizer™

The Elephant Conversation™ is essential because it requires leaders and organization members to be able to say out loud the things they disagree with within the organization. In order for this process to be productive, those involved must be open to hearing the negative, without shutting down those around them or shutting down the process. You have undoubtedly worked with these types of low emotional intelligence players before. They thrive in organizations where the status quo is good enough and the most important quality in an employee is the ability to be liked, regardless of whether that employee contributes to the growth of the organization.

People with high emotional intelligence, however, possess qualities that invite constructive feedback and turn it into meaningful change. Be on the lookout for people who:

Are difficult to offend

A trait of the emotionally intelligent player is that they are confident and have a pretty thick skin. When someone challenges an idea or process in the organization, they are open enough not to take it personally but to see the possibilities for growth.

Know their strengths and weaknesses

When someone knows and is OK with their weaknesses, it's much harder to push their buttons (or even find buttons to try to push). This allows for an open conversation, without worrying about saying the wrong thing; instead the focus is on pinpointing the problem and finding a solution.

Know how to say no

As important as it is to be open to conversations about how to move the company forward, it is just as important to know how to stay on track. An emotionally intelligent person is not prone to impulsive action and is much less susceptible to burnout. Instead, they are able to be open to others, while still maintaining healthy boundaries.

EMBRACE CHANGE

Once The Elephant Conversation™ has happened, your organization will start to implement new ways of thinking and doing things through The Momentum Accelerator™. The Momentum Accelerator™ is dedicated to identifying the right people and the right processes to begin the execution of your plan. We begin by establishing the long and short-term plans for the company. This drives accountability, performance, and alignment within the organization.

In other words, change is coming. For some, this is enough to cause a paralyzing fear that could lead to friction within the organization. You might find that those who are afraid of change lash out or only see the negative in a proposed plan. This negative feeling can change the way a team functions, affect other team members, and slow down the plan. A fear of change may even be enough to hold the company back, particularly if it manifests itself within organizational leaders. Instead, encourage your team members to be:

Flexible

Flexibility is the opposite of fear of change. Those who lack emotional intelligence may be more comfortable when their role is clearly defined and rigid. Help those around you to become comfortable with adapting to new situations.

Planners

The image of an ostrich with its head in the sand is a cliché for a reason. Our instinct is to avoid difficult and challenging changes. However, emotionally intelligent people know that change is unavoidable and when they see it coming down the pipeline, they create a plan of action to help them through it. Have a conversation with those who may be feeling fear about the company's transition and help them create a plan for their future within the organization.

EMBRACE FORWARD MOMENTUM

The last thing you want for your vision is for it to stagnate after the planning stage. Execution is key and is often the most difficult stage in any organizational change. In order to move forward and truly transform what you do and how you do it, you need people who are excited for the next step, and the next, and the next, all the way to The Value Multiplier™. Excitement, however, is difficult to maintain, particularly for those who are not self-aware enough to take an inventory of their emotional health and begin good habits to maintain it. Those that are able to walk this tight-rope are able to:

Let go of mistakes

Letting go of mistakes in no way means forgetting them. Having access to and learning from past mistakes is an important way to grow. It does mean, though, that wallowing in past mistakes is not an option. The key to maintaining a balance between remembering and learning is the resilience to get back up when you fall down.

Avoid seeking perfection: While we might all know that perfection doesn't exist, for some it is incredibly difficult to embrace that idea. But, if all we seek is perfection, we'll never be able to move forward. All our attention will be stuck on how we can make one small piece of the puzzle match up to our ideals, instead of looking at how that piece fits into the larger picture. Focusing on the excitement of what you have achieved, regardless of perfection, will allow you to become excited about what you will achieve in the future.

> Avoid seeking perfection.

Disconnect

Those with high emotional intelligence are constantly checking in with their mood, stress level, and physical health. When any of these are out of whack, they understand the importance of taking time away from their stressors (which, yes, can include work) in order to recharge and maintain their well-being.

If you can cultivate these qualities in your team, you will be well on your way to achieving your goals.

BENEFITS OF INVESTING IN YOUR LEADERSHIP TEAM

Where Are All The Transformational Leaders?

We've all worked for businesses which could be described as average; things are "okay." Things are chugging along fine, but there isn't the aura of excitement or growth that makes you want to get up in the morning and keep pushing through the mountain of emails in your inbox or continue making progress on that project that has stretched out into month six, seven, or eight. There's nothing horribly wrong with the workplace or the boss or the team; there's just the vague sense that everything at work is blah. How did it get here?

It's easy to blame management (or leadership, or both), but this is one type of issue where key influencers really can make a difference, no matter what role you fill on the Org Chart. If you are working with truly transformational leaders, it doesn't matter what direction the company is going or if it's a startup or a business that's been around for one hundred years; you will feel an exciting forward momentum, pulling you and your team along toward new goals, new ideas, and bigger growth.

Transformational Leadership Coaching

So how does company leadership get to the point at which they are truly "transformational?" It's difficult to do alone. People usually lean into their strengths and can often develop pretty intense anxieties and fears around things they don't see as their forte. A numbers person may avoid the people—"touchy-feely"—side of leadership. Or the natural salesperson may avoid dealing with the logistics needed to ensure a project's overall success. Only favoring one side of your personality is a lopsided way to lead, and sometimes you need an outside perspective to help you face the aspects of your performance you've been neglecting.

There is a strong corollary in working with someone from outside the organization and success. It's more than revealing blind spots. It's about perspective. Having a "coach in your corner" will not only help you better play to your strengths. You will also learn how to manage your weaknesses and leverage them to partner with others on the team, thereby building a well-rounded team. More than that, you will become more aware of beliefs that may be limiting you. You will also discover positive passions and learn how to tap into them to become more productive. A truly unbiased view of yourself will allow you to practice the skill and art of being a transformational leader.

THE TOP SIX "SOFT" SKILLS NEEDED TO BE AN EFFECTIVE LEADER

If you're a leader within your organization, you may have an MBA, decades of work experience, or a precocious knack for management (or maybe even all three). But sometimes, even the most prepared person needs leadership resources. Just because you have a leadership title doesn't necessarily make you an effective leader. So what does?

Fearlessness

Being at the top of any organization is scary. The success of the business and your employees' success ultimately rest on your shoulders. For many people, it's easier to focus on the purely business side of things rather than the people side of things. The business stuff, after all, is easier to control. You can use hard data to predict what will happen next and you don't have to worry if you're going to hurt the business' feelings. However, if you don't have an effective team full of people who understand and support your business ideas, your plans won't have any legs.

This is why an effective leader must be fearless in their communication with their team and with the wider corporate organization. If you want your plans for the future of your organization to be successful, then you have to make sure that

> An effective leader must be fearless in their communication with their team.

your team is on board. If there is any resistance, then you have to confront it head-on. Hopefully, a healthy dialogue about your vision will lead to a team that is full of members who will make your project successful in the long run, despite any discomfort those conversations may initially cause.

Proactiveness

If you've ever found yourself having a moment of truth with an employee or a team, you know how frustrating those conversations are and you know how stressful and unpleasant the work environment is for everyone in the weeks or months leading up to that conversation. While it's always good when dysfunction is addressed, an effective leader knows that such conversations should come early and often.

Being proactive in addressing any issues that your team has with your plan, project, or vision is the best way for you to ensure that your team is working productively. That communication also allows for you to see any real issues early so that you can make necessary changes to ensure success.

Engagement

When you are a leader, your time is precious. You're constantly being pulled in many different directions. And so, it's easy to rely just on one-way communications: email, text message, or just offering short directives. They have their place. However, nothing takes the place of connecting with people.

Proactive, fearless communication takes engagement: the

effort to give attention to people, be interested in them, and connect with them. We have a front row seat at witnessing effective leaders develop habits of intentionally connecting. They see engagement as conversation, not dictation. They slow down to create space, look people in the eye, ask questions, actively listen, and clarify what they are hearing. Beyond that, they stay connected by following up to maintain the dialogue. During the day, they also look for opportunities in casual conversations to encourage, compliment, and give insight. Engaged leaders know that every interchange is an opportunity to reiterate the vision and values, thereby creating engaged followers.

Knowing When to Lead

There is an "art" of leadership versus management. While there are many traits that point to leadership, the uniting factor of all of them is big-picture, long-term thinking. As you work with your team, bringing them on board with your plan, it's important not to forget that you are the pilot of a large ship. Being too controlling with the details or implementation of your plan will cause you to lose sight of the big-level ideas you are pursuing and to, metaphorically, crash into the rocks. Don't be afraid to delegate, inspire, and take the long view.

Knowing When to Manage

Just as it's important to not lose sight of what it means to be a leader, it is just as critical to recognize when it's time to be a manager. It might seem counterintuitive, but an effective leader can easily become a manager who provides their team with the tools it needs. Those tools might be something as immediate as the skills needed to complete projects or something as intangible as an understanding of the rules and systems the team is working within. Without these tools, the team may be fully behind your plan, but they won't be able to execute it.

Flexibility

So, you may be reading this and thinking: "Wait, you want me to be a leader and a manager? I need to delegate, but I also need to make sure I'm communicating proactively?" Yes, because an effective leader is, above all, flexible. In business, as in all things, you can't truly predict what might happen next, and as the leader, it's up to you to take these unforeseen changes in stride. It's up to you to look into your leadership toolkit and pull out the appropriate tool to keep your vision on course. Ultimately, that's what you're there for. Your team, if they're firing on all cylinders, will take care of the rest.

Ultimately, at first blush these may seem like "soft" skills. However, they are far from soft. In fact, they are quite hard. They take a level of courage and depth that is challenging. And, while the process pieces can sometimes feel simplistic, an extreme amount of discipline is required to optimize execution.

Here, we've only shared the top six skills needed to be an effective leader. There are many more that can be worked on and improved. Nexecute has helped organizations thrive by helping them learn to improve their "not-so-soft" skills.

CHAPTER 6

"My grandfather always said, 'I don't like cobwebs,' meaning that companies that don't move or change collect them. Today's world requires us to be agile and adaptable. By embracing and utilizing a dynamic planning process, we have found a lot of success in an industry that is constantly changing."

-JOSEPH BASILE, PRESIDENT

Dynamic Strategic Planning Plus Productivity

PRODUCTIVITY IN BUSINESS

Quite possibly, the most important issue those in leadership and management positions in any size business obsesses over is productivity. How can I make the business more productive? How can we become more efficient? What can I do to increase productivity?

We all understand why productivity is so critical. By getting better results in a shorter amount of time, profits should grow. Like the saying goes, "Time is money, my friend," and senior leaders know that to be all too true. So, what are ways to increase productivity?

There have been innumerable economic and psychological studies. Hundreds of books have been written on the topic of productivity alone. In fact, the business of selling productivity is probably a billion dollar industry. The reality of productivity is this: everything that truly increases productivity has already been discovered and shared. Unless a time machine ends up being invented sometime in the not-so-distant future, we've already figured out the big secrets to achieving productivity.

Getting "Lean"

In 1991, James P. Womack, Daniel T. Jones, and Daniel Roos wrote a book titled *The Machine that Changed the World*, which coined the term "lean production," derived from the Toyota Production System. The car manufacturing conglomerate in Japan developed a system that minimized waste, while identifying added value, and reducing everything else that did not add value. Put simply, it used continuous analysis and process to get the most out of the least.

Simple, right?

Not so much. How can you possibly get the most out of the least? We've identified the top three key practices to get the most out of the least, and to move from busy to productive.

THE THREE SECRETS TO PRODUCTIVITY IN BUSINESS

Become Super Focused

Focus on what's important. Identify the determining factors that make a task a priority and then make sure you cross the most important task off your list first. This is called the Ivy Lee method, and we will dive deeper into this method later in this chapter.

Do Productive Tasks, Not Busy Tasks

All too often, when there are a lot of things to do and the

priorities aren't clear, many people will either work on what's easy or the biggest fire of the moment. When they're not focusing on the things that will truly make a difference in the long run, how are they being efficient or effective? They aren't, they're only busy. This is the "go to" excuse for not being productive.

Delegate Correctly

For many in leadership and management positions, it's painful to delegate because they see it as relinquishing control. Too often, they will do tasks that can easily be handed down because they enjoy them, or they don't trust the people they can hand them off to. Either way, this creates a major roadblock in productivity.

So far, we have discussed the importance of priorities and the difference between being busy and being productive. Our final secret to productivity is something that many executives, managers, and leaders struggle with—delegation. The importance of delegation in productivity should not be underestimated.

Have you ever heard the phrase, "If you want something done right, do it yourself"? The phrase was made famous by a French dramatist who took a similar quote from the Emperor Napoleon Bonaparte. No offense to Napoleon, but he had some serious delegation issues. In fact, it's a wonder he was able to conquer almost all of Europe with that kind of attitude.

Delegation isn't just important to being productive. It is necessary. Too often, we find ourselves with too many things to get done and not enough time to do it in, simply because we refuse to relinquish power or control over certain aspects of the business. This trickles down to the rest of the team.

Don't be the Bottleneck

It's sometimes a surprise to those in leadership positions when they learn they are the cause of the decrease in productivity. Often, they don't realize that their team members are waiting on decisions, approval, more coaching, or other crucial details to keep projects moving forward. Without meaning to, those in leadership positions become

> Too often, we find ourselves with too many things to get done and not enough time to do it in, simply because we refuse to relinquish power or control over certain aspects of the business.

the bottleneck simply because they become backed up with work.

This can easily be solved by delegation. If leaders were to unload some of their tasks on others, distributing responsibility and workload, they can focus on their priorities and their productivity will increase. You just have to be willing and trusting enough to hand off those tasks.

Learning to Trust

This might be a little misleading. It's not necessarily about you learning to trust, it's about finding the right people to instill your trust and confidence. It's about choosing people you know will perform the task as you would. No, even better than you would. Chances are, there are people in your organization that can do that one task you've been refusing to delegate even better than you.

Whom do you trust? We find that people are eager to "play to their strengths" and want to make an impact. Therefore, look closely at their work and their performance. Talk to their managers and coworkers and make an informed decision to trust them to complete these delegated tasks. Many times, you'll find you have trustworthy team members who can help your productivity increase and, in turn, the productivity of the organization.

Letting Go

Delegation is about letting go. It's not easy. In fact, it's one of the hardest things a leader must do. So, it's important to understand the impact of not delegating.

If you make the choice to not delegate, you put limits on success: your success, the team's success, the project's success, and the organization's success. This may seem like an overstatement. We don't believe it is. While not delegating is limiting, delegating is expansive. It broadens the impact at multiple levels.

Let's be clear though. Letting go doesn't mean abdicating responsibility or accountability. It's quite the opposite. The first step of letting go is about making sure there are clear expectations of the task or results you are delegating. The second step is giving people the space to do the task. The third step is to provide some type of timely feedback. The fourth step is to repeat steps one through three.

PRIORITIES ARE KEY TO PRODUCTIVITY

If you want to learn how to be productive, the first step is learning how to prioritize tasks. There are a lot of factors that help determine the priority level of your task and they vary from company to company and role to role. However, one thing remains the same: if you do the most important things first, then your productivity level will increase. This is because you are completing the items that have the biggest impact on your organization. Whether those tasks are internal processes or external issues shouldn't matter. What matters is the effect those tasks will have on your business.

Now, you may have doubts. How can we be sure that the prioritized tasks will really increase our productivity and make an impact on our business? Isn't it better to do multiple things at once or get all the quick stuff out of the way first? That way you're doing more in less time. Chances are, the reason why those tasks are easy and fast is because they don't make as big an impact. But don't take our word for it. Take Ivy Lee's.

THE IVY LEE METHOD

In 1918, Charles M. Schwab, president of Bethlehem Steel Corporation and one of the richest men in the world, scheduled a simple meeting with a business consultant by the name of Ivy Lee. This meeting was a "free" consultation. In the meeting, Lee described a simple method of how to get more things done:

1. Before leaving work each day, write down only the six most important things you need to get done tomorrow.

Make sure that those six items are truly prioritized.

2. At work the next day, focus on the first task. Work on it until it is completed, then move on to the next task.

3. Whatever you didn't finish should be at the top of the list for the next day. Repeat this process every day.

This was so effective for Schwab and his executives, Schwab cut Lee a check for $25,000 (roughly $400,000 today) a mere three months after the initial meeting.

WHY DOES IT WORK?

How can writing down tasks and focusing on one at a time make such a significant impact? It hardly seems possible that something as simple as creating a list of priorities and sticking to it can be so effective. The truth is, we let a lot of little things and distractions get in our way, which will slow down our productivity. So, look at the main reasons why this simple process really works:

1. Gets you going faster – Sometimes the hardest thing about going to the gym is ... simply going to the gym. Often, you'll find that once you're there, it's much easier to get moving. Some executives will procrastinate for hours just trying to decide where to begin. The sheer number of tasks feels daunting and getting started is hard when you're not sure where to start. Having those tasks in order that day removes all that pressure.

2. Forces you to evaluate tasks and make decisions – By creating a list and assigning importance to each task, it commits you to one task. That one task should be your

absolute priority and focus. Nothing else is more important, and once you realize this, then you will become less
distracted by the smaller interruptions and move on to
tasks faster. Imposing these limits on yourself is critical to
getting things done.

3. Keeps you focused and working – Concentrating on one
task, and having your sole attention and mind set to it
yields better work. It's that simple. Although our society
loves multitaskers—by the way, neuroscience reiterates
that multitasking is a myth—it's important to focus on
one thing at a time so that task will receive your maxi-
mum effort and dedication.

SIX QUESTIONS THAT WILL HELP YOU CREATE ACHIEVABLE BUSINESS GOALS

When creating your strategic plan, it's important to include
goals that you can work toward. In a lot of ways, goals are like
turning points in your business. When a goal is met, it means
you've reached a new height in your business, which sometimes
requires important decisions and actions to be taken to grow
your business further or take it into a brand-new direction.

And possibly most importantly, setting goals encourages
the entire team to come together to beat those goals. Goals
create drive for the entire company and help push the team to
meet their potential and exceed expectations.

But let's level set. Just creating any goal won't achieve the
desired effect you want. You should make sure they are realistic
and attainable, while also being strategic. When creating your
goals, ask yourself these questions:

Is the goal relevant?

The temptation is to get busy setting a goal, without asking and answering the important question, "Why?" Why is this goal important? What will it mean for the growth of my company? Without this initial discipline, you may end up setting goals that don't align to the company's long-term vision or priorities. You could end up being busy without being productive. We've learned that priority driven goals are relevant.

Is this goal realistic?

With the current team and resources, can I achieve this goal? Look carefully at where you are in the company's life cycle and the culture you're working in. Don't set goals that don't make sense for where you are. Set goals that will help you reach the point where those dream goals are achievable. At the same time, be sure that you set goals that will stretch people, thereby allowing them the opportunity to achieve more than they might initially think. Also, establishing a realistic time frame is critical. Be clear about deadlines, resources, and capabilities.

What could prevent me from achieving this goal?

It will be of no surprise that you will stumble on some hurdles and face some challenges both inside and outside of the organization. Your strengths may even unveil a weakness. This is the point where leaders define reality and honestly evaluate what can impede or maybe even stop you from achieving the goal. A good SWOT (Strengths, Weaknesses, Opportunities, Threats) exercise can help everyone face the reality, and then allow you to honestly establish a plan that ensures success.

What are the action steps, milestones, and accountabilities to achieve this goal?

Setting a goal without coming up with a plan to achieve it is like setting yourself up for failure. Take time to ensure a goal is met by figuring out what needs to happen to turn it into reality. Two key components are measurements and accountability. Metrics are a tool to help you measure successes to celebrate and reveal deterrents to correct. As we've mentioned earlier, "the core of accountability is commitment, a willingness to be held accountable and hold others accountable."

You've met the goal, now what?

First, celebrate! (Don't forget this.) Then you have a choice: stagnate or move forward. Our guess is that you want to take it to the next level. Since you have a proven pattern of achieving your goals that work, the next step is to repeat the process. Implement the plan again by aligning to the long-term vision. No matter the vision, ensure you accomplish it by executing the plan.

If this goal is not met, how do I rebound?

Not reaching your goal is not the end of the world. It just means you have more to learn. Evaluate your mistakes. Look at what worked (celebrating the smaller wins) and what didn't. Then set a more achievable goal next time. The worst thing you can do is just ignore it. Einstein's words are true, "Insanity is doing something over and over again and expecting the same result." Therefore, we need to learn from our mistakes. Analyze the root cause and spend the time asking the tough questions: What didn't we anticipate? Did someone drop the ball on an assignment? Were there a series of poor decisions? Was the wrong person held accountable for a task? Is the wrong person on the team?

Asking yourself these six questions can help you set goals that allow your company to reach new heights. But if you still need some help setting those goals and coming up with ones that will be effective long term, consider hiring a business consultant and they will ensure you not only have great goals, but beat them as well!

CREATE A STRATEGIC PLAN THAT WORKS FOR YOUR BUSINESS

You have a spectacular business. Your product is top-of-the-line, and your service is top-notch. Business is steady but not growing as fast or as stable as in the past. Does it have something to do with your team? Or, are your processes not as efficient or as effective as they have the potential to be?

Maybe your business is booming and growing rapidly. How can you handle that growth? What happens when you become too big to fulfill orders on time or manage client expectations?

Sometimes it's easy to get lost in the details of the business. You can become very tactical, often losing sight of the bigger picture. You can get wrapped up in things like worrying about this one person, or that particular product, or a small memo. These all beg questions like, "Where is your business going? When you do move forward? How does your business shift and adjust to meet that growth?"

It all starts with a dynamic, strategic plan.

For the very reasons stated above, a strategic plan is

necessary for your business. You need to know where you're headed and have points, processes, goals, and steps to help you get there. Without those things, you're wandering blind in a competitive business world with your employees and clients relying on you.

So how do you go about creating a strategic plan? Depending on the type of business, there's practically an infinite number of ways. But we can tell you for sure what every business plan must be. Your plan must be:

Actionable

People talk and talk about creating a plan, and when they finally do, they just let it sit there. What point is there in having a plan if you don't follow through with it? Use it! Execute it! Your business won't go anywhere without you implementing change that has been designed strategically to help it.

Flexible

You constantly hear about how fast things change in your industry. Technology has changed our world. Rapid changes in technology force rapid changes in the business environment, sometimes causing our goals to become obsolete. So, how are you accounting for that? Is your plan flexible and dynamic enough to accommodate these changes? If new technology is introduced, can you take time to learn and implement that technology before losing ground to your competitors or market? Or, what if your business hinges on something that constantly fluctuates, like the price of oil or the housing market? It also may be something more internal, where you lose an important member of your team or a process stops working for whatever reason.

When creating your plan, consider all external and internal factors and design a plan that accounts for all of them. Furthermore, ensure you have a process in place that allows for tactical changes as needed to ensure the long-term goals are met.

Trackable

To make sure you are following through with your plan, it's helpful to set goals (more on this to come) and keep track of your progress. Take note! Who is working the plan? What's working in your plan? What's not? Take advantage of the flexibility you've built into your plan and make adjustments to capitalize on those successes.

Keep track of where you are in your plan and how far you need to go. Have you reached your quarterly objectives? How are your daily decisions aligning to the long-term goals? Have you implemented the new process you have in place once you reached a certain capacity? What about hiring that new manager when you exceeded [x] amount of clients? Knowing where you are in your plan will help you continue to move forward and stay on track.

Accountable

Here's the key: it's a mistake to track the plan without accountability. We find that a lack of accountability is the failing piece of any plan. At the core of accountability is commitment. There must be a willingness to be held accountable and hold others accountable.

Accountability isn't about being mean, ruthless, or unbending. Rather, it is the piece that does the heavy lifting in meeting your goals. At the outset, it sets the stage for who is responsible for each part of the plan and who is holding that person accountable. During the process, the metrics will drive the next accountable actions.

> It's a mistake to track the plan without accountability.

To be sure, accountability requires commitment and without it, nothing gets done. The best way to ensure you meet these criteria in your strategic business plan is to hire a business advisor who understands your industry and your clients, and is more than willing to join you on your path to business success.

WHAT MAKES YOU PRODUCTIVE?

Productive team members can properly prioritize their tasks. We know that the Ivy Lee method suggested prioritizing a list of six things. We would suggest that you get even more focused and choose fewer items to be more productive.

When looking at your day, week, month, quarter, year, or life, ask this question, "If I could only do three to five things today (or this week, month, quarter, etc.), what would take me further than anything else toward reaching my goal?" If leaders could build habits around this type of thinking, then their own forward motion and that of their companies would yield greater results.

What's the Real Priority?

It's no surprise that under different situations, different types of priorities might be chosen. In some situations, leaders may make the wrong decisions on priorities, thus having a negative long-term effect on their company.

A leadership mindset means that the leader is focused on results. That means starting with the end in mind and working backwards. Honestly ask, "What result do I want to see?"

Once you are clear on the results, determine three to five manageable actions that you can put into place. Prioritize the tasks from one to five. Of course, the first tasks are the most important tasks that will drive you to your results. They are the ones that will create the most impact. They may or may not take the most time. Remember, the issue is to define tasks that make you productive.

Being Productive?

Now it's time to get to work, starting with task one. Don't let the busyness of the day or others' perception of your busyness sway you. Don't forget, you have made the right decision to follow the order of your list to be productive. Tomorrow, and every day after that, you can make a similar decision. Now, you are on your way to develop a habit of being productive.

CHAPTER 7

"Having transformational conversations ultimately builds deeper levels of trust."

-TIM O'HALLA, PRESIDENT AND CEO

Discovering Needs

DISCOVERING THE PROBLEM: IS IT THE CHICKEN OR THE EGG?

There are so many ways you can approach finding a problem, and many different entry points. One of the ways we can look at it is, "Is it the chicken or is it the egg?" When we're talking to a client the first time, we're really trying to understand what their needs are. Is it a team or people issue? Or is it a process issue? Usually, it is both. So where do you start?

If your team is highly dysfunctional, that's where you need to start. In over eighteen years, we have only met one company with a fully functional team. It's not that working on process is easier, it is that working on process can help identify dysfunctional parts of the team. A big part of that process is identifying the core values. About one third of the time, a client will tell us, "We already have core values. We don't need to do anymore work on it." There are two kinds of CEOs that we work with. There is the kind that thinks they know the problem and they are ready to get into it, and there is the CEO that thinks they know the problem but has their head buried in the sand.

In either event, by starting on instilling processes that drive accountability and results, it becomes obvious where the problem lies. The problems could be related to broken processes that need to be fixed, but more often than not, the problems lie with people on the executive team. Sometimes the role has outgrown the person, while other times there is a core values mismatch. In either event, a tough decision needs to be made and that decision is typically that the person must be moved off the team (either into another role or out of the company). This can be particularly difficult if the person has been there a long time and is well liked, but it is necessary. If we begin working on the people side of things with the wrong people on the team, we won't be able to get the team to full functionality. It's essential to have everyone on the team to have the potential to be part of a fully functioning team to be successful. This becomes a key first step in building a culture of accountability and results. The truth is that, on average, 15 percent of the executives on the executive teams we work with don't survive the first six months and as much as 50 percent don't survive the first year. This may seem extreme, but people cannot hide when you raise the visibility of data and start holding the right people accountable for performance. Please understand, this is a healthy part of growth and gives a CEO the opportunity to raise the performance of their team.

We can go in with the premise of process because process will show where there is conflict in a dysfunctional team.

The reality is that leaders often need to face the truths

about where their own processes have failed and where their team's alignment with their core values may have either not been firmly established or needs to be reinvigorated.

About 90 percent of the time, when that occurs, an hour later they're ready to throw their core values in the garbage and start over. Often, they come to realize that they've gone through an artificial process initially, where they sat around and picked words that sounded nice but weren't necessarily the true core values of the organization. Once they've reassessed their core values, almost always, they realize there are members of their executive team that are not in line with their core values.

> The reality is that leaders often need to face the truths about where their own processes have failed.

You've got two competing philosophies out there in the world. One is, if you've got great people, nothing else matters, because organizational health trumps everything else. Great people, even if they have bad processes, will still generate success. The other is, if you have great processes you don't need great people, because great processes will drive success. Both of those statements are a combination of truth and lie all in one. Back to the original question, is it the chicken or the egg?

One thing that seems to occur is that people get hung up on the people issues, and don't want to face the process issues. We've had clients say, "We don't want strategy. We don't need to review the processes. We just need to fix the people." We can promise you that the process is probably broken. We can help with working the people side of it, no question, but in cases where the leadership doesn't recognize a process problem, we'll probably never address it. The company will never quite get the performance that they could because there is a lack of accountability for all of the pieces. We know that companies do strategic planning, but if it's an underlying processes issue, they'll never get to address it with a mindset like that.

For example, we worked with a particular client for a quite a while, and it was nearly impossible to get the company to wrap their minds around the process stuff. We'd done amazing work around the company on team dynamics, but they kept making "stupid" mistakes—ones that were a simple fix that they repeated regularly. There were parts of the company that were functioning very well, parts that we were working with, and parts that weren't functioning very well. The bigger issue is that because they didn't have a consistent, clear process driven toward execution, the issues weren't flagged all at once. It takes the leaders stepping up and saying, "No, we have to keep this going and this is why." Real leaders never stop trying to improve all facets of their company because they know anything built on a faulty foundation is not built to last.

It's a funny thing. If we start with the process, it's easy to bring the people part into check within a year. But when we start with the people, it seems very difficult, to nearly impossible, to get the process part going.

People confuse us with strategic planners, which we are not. No one has a word yet for what we do on the process side of it, so it falls into this bucket of strategic planning, and a lot of these leaders have a perception of what strategic planning is. Some of it is positive and some of it is negative. But it's just not strategic planning. Strategic planning is 1 percent of the work that we do, if that. It's really about execution and we do that through a combination of implementing processes and people.

We've also had a large organization, approximately a $150 million division of a multibillion dollar company, say, "We really want the organizational health process, but we can't have your processes portion because I'm trying to create a healthy team right here." The challenge is, if his VP and president don't buy into that, they could squelch the whole thing in a matter of weeks, and that's exactly what ended up happening. You need to be able to have the people at the top involved with and believing in the process.

Typically, organizational leaders want to start with their strategic plan. They don't often want to focus on the effectiveness of their team, believing they have assembled a great team of people. We would refocus them on execution and not just the "plan." By instilling processes that drive accountability and results, it often becomes very obvious that they have problems with their people. It is so obvious, in fact, that the leader cannot ignore it any longer. Now, we can focus on the people part of the equation, which is at the root of the culture.

The right process and the right people matter. As an example, without the point of view of someone who is focused on the people side of the equation, when there are people issues, some may think the easiest solution is just "fire them all." The truth of it is that most CEOs tend NOT to fire people in a timely manner. Once they finally make the choice to remove members of the team that don't fit, they always wish they had done it sooner.

It's easy to build a process-based team that functions fairly well from a process and execution perspective, but does not function well from a relationship perspective. The part that you can never account for in that situation is what someone could do, or the possibility. They might be performing okay, and the company has been growing 5 percent to 6 percent every year. Everybody's happy. Everyone's getting a bonus. But could they have grown 20 percent or 25 percent?

There was a company we started working with a couple of years ago. The CEO found us through networking, and we went and met with her and her team. These were excellent leaders who had a few issues on their team, like anyone else might. They were performing decently; however, their goal was to sell the company in a few years and they wanted to really maximize the value of their company. More often than not, the way that people try to drive up the value when they are trying to sell their company is they cut a lot, with the hope that the company will sell quickly. Most investors see that. Making those cuts can actually hurt the value of a company, so it can have a backfire effect. These guys were too smart for that, but they just felt like they weren't maximizing. At that particular time, they'd gone out to a test market and a number of investment groups. They were looking at somewhere in the neighborhood of two to maybe four time multiple against their EBIT (Earnings Before Interest and Taxes).

From a financial standpoint, when you are selling your company, any interest you pay to a bank, any taxes you've paid, and any depreciation or amortization are all considered "add backs." They take the bottom line profitability of a company, add those things back, and come up with an earnings-based model that says, "This is our true, actual cash earnings of the company for one year." And then, most of the time, it will sell for a multiple of that.

We came in and started working with them. We ended up having to change the CEO of one of their divisions and swap a few people out. In the primary company, though, we didn't change anyone. Frankly, the teams were pretty high-functioning. They didn't need much help on the people side of it, they just needed some cleanup. They sold last year for ten times their EBIT to a strategic buyer.

Leaders have to run their company like they aren't going to sell. This company increased their top line and bottom line because they focused on the most important issues of culture and execution by utilizing The Results Optimizer™.

A high percentage of the time, the person that brings us in is flexible and ready for a change. There are some caveats to that. Usually we get hired at the CEO level. It's very rare otherwise, and we don't even engage in discussions unless the CEO is involved in most cases. For our process to work, there has to be someone in charge who can drive it, a leader who is totally on board.

When we get to the team, after about six to twelve months, 30 percent to as high as 50 percent of the executive team does not survive the process, as an average. There have been exceptions though. In the case of one company, in a team of about ten people, there are only three of them there now who were original members. That's 70 percent that didn't make it. But then, we'll have a company where there was only one out of seven or eight that didn't make it.

We are upfront with potential clients about this phenomena. Here is a section of our proposal letter:

"A word of caution, though. As we build habits and drive performance; as accountability, alignment, and team health begin to drive behaviors; and as the company begins to accelerate into the future, sometimes people are lost. Inevitably, this process highlights some individuals that are not up to the challenge. Those individuals may not continue in their current role. In our opinion, either is fine, as these types of people hold companies back. It is important, though, for us to highlight this potential, as some leaders aren't able to handle these types of changes."

When we are doing the work on the process and grading people, it's a fairly high percentage of people on the executive team that won't make it. Sometimes it's not the obvious people who are causing the issue. It's amazing how often the CEO is shocked by which people's behaviors are uncovered by the system. Again, if they have the core values, we don't want to lose them if we can change behaviors. When we work with a company, on average, 30 percent to 50 percent of the members of the executive team don't survive the first year of our processes.

> When we work with a company, on average, 30 percent to 50 percent of the members of the executive team don't survive the first year of our processes.

One leader asked us, "When am I going to be able to have a steady team? When will I get to stop replacing people?" The truth is if you are growing as a company, people are going to come and go. It is just part of the process.

One of our first clients is still a client today and we have been working with them for over fifteen years. They have seventeen people on their executive team. Only three of the people of the seventeen were there when we started. Of the other fourteen positions, several of them have turned over a couple of times. Some of that is owing to the fact that they are growing and sometimes people can get them from point A to point B, but can't get them to point C. But most of the turn-over has been because of core values mis-hiring.

When we came in, they had a COO who was ready to retire and was one of the most wonderful people you will ever meet. He was completely aligned to the core values. The company was also at a stage where it was beginning to grow beyond his skills. He saw this as an opportunity to help find his replacement and leave with grace. He had grown up in the company learning all of his skills on the job. While great at his position, the company need something more to enter its next phase of growth. The added capacity required greater operational skill. He stayed on for about another year to aid with the transition

We give these companies the tools they need to hire based on their skills and their core values. When we were working with them, they had engaged a separate recruiting firm to help them hire their new COO. We had a very big philosophical disagreement on behavioral interviewing. Instead of digging deep, and interviewing based on our advice, they sent an email to the three biggest candidates and said, "Here are the core values of the agency. Tell us how you exhibit these core values in your day-to-day life." We would never take this approach.

This, in our opinion, gives every candidate the opportunity to lie, or at least give an impression that they have the core values.

What they got were three candidates who were able to answer these questions about the core values in such a way that they all looked like they had the core values. They gave the candidates the opportunity to lie. Since it seemed as if everyone had the core values, they chose the candidate with the best skills, and in two years time, the new COO totally crashed and burned. The lack of true behavioral interviewing failed to determine if the candidate truly had the core values. That wasn't the only problem, though. They also failed to truly validate whether the person really had the kills to execute the position. They hired the person who interviewed best and ended up with a person who had the wrong core values, creating all kinds of problems within the organization. Ultimately, they had to fire this person and start over.

On the next effort, we were hammering core values at all levels of the interview process. Even the best interviewing process isn't always foolproof. Again, we had a few candidates, all with some level of alignment to the core values. The company's leadership ended up hiring the one who they liked the most. This person was pretty solidly aligned with three out of the five core values, but the other two were really questionable. At this point, the organization as a whole were driving the concept of core values alignment pretty hard and about six months after she was hired, the new COO came in and announced, "This isn't working for me," and left. It seemed crazy at the time because she really did have good skills, and the company really did think she had enough alignment to the core values. This was right on the heels of having a meeting about the core values and what they meant for the organization. She quit when we made it clear how serious we were about the core values.

We often get asked the question when companies are hiring, "Do they have to have all the core values?" The answer is "yes" and this story is an example why. The real question the leader should be asking is, "Which core value are we willing to sacrifice or isn't as important as the others?" If there are core values that aren't as important or we are willing to "bend" on them, then we have the wrong core values.

This isn't just the dynamic of, "I hate my job." Let's say they went to school and became an IT specialist. They worked their way up and became either an IT manager or even a CTO in their organization. Hating their job can look like one of two things. They still love IT but they hate their job, and that hate is directly related to their environment. That is a core values issue 95 percent of the time. They jump ship and go to another company where they have similar core values and now love their job, still doing accounting. That's when it's not skills based.

The second are those people who truly hate the job they do. They hate certain aspects of IT, or specific nuances of it. Now we are starting to get into some other dynamics. Maybe they aren't doing work aligned to their uniqueness.

Do you see how easy it is for process work to move into people work? This is what drew the two of us together in the first place.

By the way, the third time was a charm. Finally, our client was ready to ensure a complete core values fit. It took much longer, getting to the point of frustrating, but when the right person was found, it was obvious he had all the core values. He was hired and helped them break through operational barriers that were holding them back. As of the writing of this book, he is still there and generating success.

 We see execution and culture as a Yin and Yang: driving execution and results, while at the same time transforming leaders and teams. It is a harmonious approach, which is why the tagline of this book is, "Results happen when culture meets execution."

Because self-awareness is the first component of transformational leaders, we consistently challenge leaders to become mindful, conscious, and aware of who they are. We encourage them to grow in an ever-deepening understanding of their own personalities, instincts, strengths, weaknesses, emotions, and drives.

If you are working contrary to your instincts, it creates a strain. For instance, if you're free-spirited and you don't like a lot of structure but you're working in a role where structure matters all the time, you are going to hate it. If you are a summary person and you are in a role where you are continuously gathering data, that's going to drive you crazy. There are other indicators, but the place you have to start is: Is it the job or is it the environment? If it's the environment, then it is really the core values and some other personality conflicts. If it is specifically the work, then it is probably relating more to your instincts and strengths.

Here's an example. We were engaged to work with an executive leadership team. They had been clients for a number of years and they were clear on their core values and actively engaged in executing successful results quarter after quarter. They were functioning as a team; however, driving execution and accountability started showing some levels of team dysfunction, especially as the bar for performance was raised. To get back on track, the president wanted to challenge them to become a more cohesive, higher-performing team, which meant they needed to learn how to become even better leaders. We knew that it had to start with self-awareness and building even deeper levels of trust. So, with a series of exercises, we helped the team identify their strengths, weaknesses, and natural inclinations. Within the first twenty minutes, they knew their positive contributions and talents and learned how to define them and process how they engaged with them. Their team would now be in a better position to propel forward on the individual strengths they each brought to the table, rather than having any role or task misalignment taking them away from their goals.

As part of the process, we ask them to consider two questions, "What would it mean if I took the time to learn about my talents and develop and invest in them? And, what would inhibit me from doing so?" During the break, one member of that executive team came up and shared with us his answer. It was simply, "I would quit my job." That's an extreme example but it's completely true. This process opens the door for people to ask the deeper questions they may have never asked before.

That's why we talk about all four pillars of culture, not just the pillar of results. One might assume that you can achieve sustainable results without having people engaged or working in a trusting environment, but you cannot. Senior leaders need to ask brutally honest questions like, "What is inhibiting me or my team from growing? What will propel me and my team forward to success? Do I have a well-rounded team that is invigorated by what they do? Does my team build strategic partnerships or work in silos? Are we a healthy or a dysfunctional team? Do we hold each other accountable?"

CHAPTER 8

"Achieving success takes a lot of time and patience. A leader must be dedicated to building the right culture, meaning that they have the right people, the right goals and everyone is aligned. When everyone knows what has to be done, they don't have to be managed. Results happen."

-Tiffany Amorosino, Chief Executive Officer

When It Works

We believe in a relentless pursuit of flawless execution. Well aware that flawless execution may be illusive, we want to engage with a realistic optimism that we can help organizations move in that direction. Therefore, structures and processes are essential for people to engage at a level where this pursuit is possible.

We meet all types of leaders with different personalities, talents, and backgrounds. It is a gift when we get to work with the ones who are committed to an execution culture. They are passionate and humble leaders who know they don't have all the answers, but are willing to learn and will lean on the expertise of others. They have tenacity to practice what we call the SMART and STRONG parts of an organization.

What does it look like when it works? Here are just a few ways we see the successes of transformational leaders:

- They face challenges head-on. It is a misconception that by practicing the principles outlined in this book, challenges will decrease. Rather, because of growth, challenges may increase and, for that matter, be of greater weight. That is the nature of business in an ever-changing world.

- They follow the process. Because they have seen the process work, they are committed to following it. They see the temptations to get lazy for what they are: temptations. So, they are more committed than ever to making sure that the strategy is executed.

- They create something sustainable. We have yet to meet an executive who doesn't want to build a sustainable organization. However, we meet plenty of them who are not willing to do the hard work. It's our privilege to work with those who are willing to build a legacy that will live well beyond their tenure at the organization.

- They build teams that are nimble in the face of market challenges. There are times that market dynamics or customer needs create unforeseen shifts. If the foundation of the organization is solid and plans are dynamic, they can navigate the unexpected and still thrive.

- They operate at levels of trust. Trust intentionally becomes a regular topic of conversations and trainings. They assure trust is practiced. And, when they see a breakdown in trust, they assure that conflict is addressed, not avoided or circumvented.

- They invest in their people. They take personal and professional development seriously, thereby building transformational leaders at every level. They make sure training is practical and results-focused.

- They create space for people to thrive and live out their passion and giftedness, even if it means helping others exit their organization because that person has a desire to pursue a different role in a different organization.

At this point, you may be questioning what the ROI is on spending so much time working on this stuff. What would it mean to you to have a highly functioning team and culture that was generating optimal results? Though we have had many clients tell us it has been invaluable, and they would still be stuck or seeing downward results by not doing this work, here are some numbers we have experienced.

- For companies who are looking for sales growth, we have seen sales grow by 1.5x to 2.5x in the first year and as much as 5x over the next three years.

- We have seen double-digit growth in Net Promotor Scores for companies that are highly focused on customer centricity.

- Initially, turnover can go up as we identify some individuals that aren't a good fit for the company early on. With implementing better hiring practices and the creation of a better culture with more engaged employees, we have seen turnover rates fall by 50 percent to as high as 87 percent.

- EBIT growth rates have been significant in many of our companies. For our really big clients, even a small EBIT gain can mean a lot of money, but with our middle market companies, we typically see double-digit increases within two to five years, depending on their industry and size.

Though results can certainly vary, the truth is that disciplined transformational leaders generate high-performing cultures and that has a definite return on investment of the time allocated and dedicated to building these cultures.

> Disciplined transformational leaders generate high-performing cultures and that has a definite return on investment.

CHAPTER 9

"The biggest difference in our performance came when we got our team right. This meant that we had to make some tough changes and have some hard conversations. Once we had the right people on our team, we ensured that everyone was working within their strengths. Our results began to accelerate at a faster pace than we expected."

-Jason Christensen, Chief Executive Officer

Who Is on Your Team?

When Abe Lincoln talked about spending hours sharpening an ax before cutting down a tree, it was a metaphor for preparation.

At each and every stage in a leadership process, preparation and then execution (followed by follow-up), is key. We've talked a lot about the importance of execution, but it's also critical to test theory and processes and discuss philosophy with trusted advisors.

Some organizations get together and review the best practices of others.

How do other leaders ensure they gain knowledge about best practices? One company has created a consortium of owners within their industry.

Daseke Inc., built by entrepreneur Don Daseke, has a network of trucking company fleet owners that meets at least once a year to review best practices.

No matter what you do to gain wisdom and knowledge, it's important to develop a process that involves collaboration with external advisors.

TRUSTED BUSINESS ADVISORS CAN REINVIGORATE YOUR TEAM

Once you've gained wisdom about what others are doing better, and what best practices you can incorporate into your own processes and organization, the real challenge begins! Incorporating advice into your own team requires great planning and execution. Once you know where you want to go, it's time to sharpen the ax even more. This is a point of frustration for many leaders and a crossroads where some can get stuck.

Execution can slow down when there's too much information, or complexity. Overanalysis can cause a complete shutdown in execution but so can lack of information or the wrong information. This is where a trusted advisor comes in.

Earlier in this book, we discussed in great length the importance of team compatibility and using the good synergy a team produces to follow established business processes. When these business processes are

> Execution can slow down when there's too much information, or complexity.

followed and the plan is actually executed, we achieve those long-awaited results. Using trusted business advisors to get an outsider's perspective can be incredibly useful.

Easier said than done.

Of course, Jim Collins backed up this philosophy with the book Good to Great when he told leaders what every consultant knows: Get the right people on the bus and the wrong people off. Once that step has been taken, leaders may feel a sense of relief. But what's next? Now is the time to create a sustainable plan and execute it.

BUILDING TRANSFORMATIONAL TEAMS

We understand that building transformational teams is a difficult task, to say the least. As the leader, you have a lot of weight on your shoulders. It's obvious that your success depends on results, but it's not always clear that it involves managing a team that is underperforming for whatever reason. Unfortunately, being able to take a step back and objectively see the reason or multiple reasons that the team is struggling with execution is not something a leader can always do, no matter how good they are. It's the same for discussing personal and strategic growth with an individual. A leader leads, and it can be hard to see the forest for the trees. Leaders themselves need the support of others.

How then can a leader begin to unravel the complexities of individuals and teams to achieve results? Our position is that you don't have to. Creating more stress on a leader is not always the answer. Stepping back and shifting your focus to a different project while allowing an external voice to evaluate and assess the next steps can breathe new life and energy into every aspect of the organization.

This isn't giving up. This isn't admitting fault, or taking a delay. It's simply doing what every expert, master, or professional sports team and organization has done.

It's not meant to sound discouraging, just realistic. Every leader needs a coach and a trusted advisor to bounce ideas off of and help execute great plans. Winston Churchill, Steve

Jobs, and Elon Musk. Not one executed their vision alone.

Even the best leaders are often overwhelmed by other responsibilities and may be too close to the problem to see the solution. That's why we often suggest enlisting the help of an outsider trained in business development and strategic execution.

Individuals do this in their own lives, with counselors or psychologists or mentors, so why not inside their organization? There can be no doubt that external advisors help stir up and create change. Sometimes it's simply a matter of putting the puzzle pieces together.

Earlier on, we discussed "How Your Team Dynamics are Holding Your Company Back."

We covered the pressures of a leader to succeed, their struggles with team cohesiveness and compatibility, strategic planning versus strategic execution, and the signature "roadblock employee" that brings down team morale.

When we discussed the "Five Tips on How to Manage Dysfunctional Teams" inside a company, some of those tips included identifying that there is a problem, communicating effectively with your team, and realizing that not all team members are a good fit, so you can build a transformational team. Hopefully that was some good information to take your teams to the next level. But if you want to go deeper and really seek transformational change in your organization, you might want to consider an outside perspective. The goal of every great leader we've encountered is to seek expertise to help sharpen their saw.

THE IMPORTANCE OF THE
IMPARTIAL THIRD PARTY

When was the last time you infused your team with the perspective of impartial advisors?

If the answer is never, now is the time. The external advisor isn't a voice of change and isn't there because you don't already have the best talent. Again, they may be the lone voice in the wilderness that can see the one thing you can't, in order to make one simple shift that accelerates results.

There's a reason why interior designers, coaches, editors, and consultants exist. It's because sometimes you need someone to be impartial. You need a trained eye, with valuable experience, to take a step back and point out what you can't see for yourself. For instance, an interior designer would be able to say those curtains, with that couch, is throwing off the whole balance of the room. But you don't see how those colors or patterns on those curtains are offsetting because you see those curtains every day. You live with them. A trusted business advisor can give you the insight you need in this situation.

Whether you engage your team or someone else, step back and make that decision to bring in experts who can bring new life to the organization by helping you challenge, accelerate, and execute.

Take this challenge today.

Hiring a team of trusted business advisors in order to benefit from an outside perspective gives you one less thing to stress over. It frees up time and valuable emotional energy. Granted, performing at optimal levels of execution and still achieving those results will always be a lot of work, but getting some extra help and advice is a stress reliever.

Leaders have enough to do and enough to worry about, and shouldn't let obsessing over your team's dynamics be one of them.

At Nexecute, we have built several programs that will help you with the goal of achieving your transformational, results-achieving team.

The programs are two phases of what we call The Results Optimizer™

This isn't just a fancy term we've created, but the best way to define what we aim to do, and it's based on decades of hard work and rolling up our sleeves inside organizations.

Every organization needs to optimize results. What's the best way? There's no magic pill. You cannot "optimize" if there's a giant mess in front of you. First, you've got to untangle, define, and evaluate without slowing down execution. The best time to focus is when there is "too much" to do. By focusing on what's most important, the greatest level of productivity can be reached. Of course, there is only so much time available, so, we must also identify what isn't a priority and what doesn't get done now.

First, it starts with what we call The Elephant Conversation™, which is exactly what it implies.

We're all aware of the elephant in the room but nobody wants to talk about it. It's uncomfortable and tense but often having that conversation helps you overcome what's been holding you back. We provide an open and easy dialogue to ensure perfect clarity to help you move forward.

Once those issues are out in the open, we undergo The Momentum Accelerator™. This tool allows you to align the right processes with the right people in the right team. With the plan in place, we help determine the key performers who will guarantee those results.

You don't need a third party to tell you how great you are and you don't need a third party to delay execution. When we go into a company, we realize that we are more than business consultants. Our leaders become your friends.

We take an advisory role with employees and teams and leaders, offering a hands-on approach to ensure the organizations we work with have the tools to achieve success. We have developed many tools to help facilitate the changes required to be made, but our approach is totally customizable based on the needs of a client. As they like to ask, "Why would you use a hammer when a screwdriver is more appropriate for the task?"

When we go into any business, we ask the hard questions:

- "Is the organization actually in trouble and why?"

- "Are there challenges that are being ignored?"

- "What is the actual truth about your team?"

- "Are you or members of your executive team truly willing to make the tough decisions to move the company forward?"

- "Are you really letting go of making all the decisions, rather than holding your team accountable for their performance and expected results?

Our role is to help leaders find the issues underneath the problems—the root issues. To do this, everyone must commit to a level of courage and honesty that may be uncomfortable.

As pretty as a plan is, if there aren't steps that people within the organization can understand and execute, then the plan is pointless.

Lastly, we will never sacrifice the long-term health or goals of a company for quick, cheap fixes. Just like a home that is built with poor planning, poor foresight, and cheap materials will crumble at the first sign of a strong wind (if it ever gets built at all), a company without a focus on the future will stumble at the first hurdle and slide back into old, unprofitable habits. Daily decisions will be made for the moment that could either impede progress or, worse yet, take the company off target in achieving the long-term goals. This can be catastrophic.

> Never sacrifice the long-term health or goals of a company for quick, cheap fixes.

WHO ARE WE AND WHERE DO WE COME FROM?

Here's a little more about us and our line of thinking.

CHRIS' STORY AND TRUTH

My dad and his siblings grew up during the Great Depression, and true to that generation, were hard-working and determined. They applied themselves and found success in the restaurant and food manufacturing business. I was one of over thirty family members and long-term employees who were like family who became part of the business my dad and his brothers built, called Big Boy Restaurants, Inc.

It is estimated that over 70 percent of all businesses are family run or family managed. However, less than 35 percent survive to see the next generation. As someone from the second generation of a family business, I learned the difference between failure and success early on. First of all, I had to learn my place in the business. Having the "right" last name put me in the family but not necessarily "in" the business. When it came to business, for me, it didn't mean special treatment. In fact, it made me a bit suspect. So, I had to learn early on in the family business to work really hard and face reality, whether at headquarters, in a restaurant, or with franchise owners domestically and internationally. These experiences shaped the importance of having a servant heart and as a young leader, how to empower the expertise of others.

As my role in leadership grew, I had to learn how to coach others and engage in healthy conflict. There were many strong personalities that needed to be navigated, and I found myself in a position where it was more important to coordinate efforts and motivate people, as opposed to being the expert with every answer. I discovered that data doesn't lie and the most important stuff must happen first. These were things I first learned from my dad early in life. I learned how to lead, instead of manage. Of course, this came with the burden of making some really tough decisions, but that all shaped me into what I am today. Along the way, there were many blessings to enjoy and many challenges to endure. What I learned most of all was the only way to survive is to live in and speak the truth.

MARK'S STORY AND TRUTH

I was raised in southwest Michigan in a pastor's family, having a front row seat in watching my dad grow a successful congregation (in reality, a non-profit organization). He was able to work with many different types of people as he grew a large church. It gave me a unique insight into the inner workings and nuances of nonprofit organizations. One challenge is learning how to create healthy boundaries. Nonprofit leaders have a strong desire to serve. Yet, it was very difficult for them (my dad) to have honest conversations. His philosophy was, "Kill 'em with kindness!" With a smile on his face, I watched him avoid confrontation. Working to keep the peace was exhausting and demanded most of his emotional energy. It was exacerbated by my mom's family mantra, "What will people think?" This is a lethal combination when it comes to facing the truth. Rather than having personal self-confidence and enjoying individuality, most of the energy is spent scanning for approval and seeking artificial harmony.

In an effort to please people, conflict was essentially negated and ultimately avoided. Psychologists repeatedly expound the virtues of conflict. It is the seedbed for interdependency, building healthy relationships. Michael Batshaw writes, "Engaging in conflict isn't going to end the relationship, it's avoiding the conflict [that might]" (*51 Things You Should Know Before Getting Engaged*). Conflict was such a touchpoint in my family that a mandate was handed down, "We will have no more conflict." The result was that truth was at best avoided and at worst, subverted.

I began my career as a pastor with that mentality. However, it didn't serve me well and limited my influence as a leader. It was a challenging journey to learn a healthier approach to life and leadership. I had to unlearn many things I had learned. This is why I am so committed to the principles of transformational leadership. They were a game changer for me. They are more than an idea. Transformational leadership is the philosophy around which I orient my life.